PANORAMAS

OTHER BOOKS BY THE AUTHOR

Papo Got His Gun
Snaps
Mainland
Tropicalization
By Lingual Wholes
Rhythm, Content & Flavor
Red Beans

EDITED BY

STUFF: A Collection of Student Writing with Herbert Kohl
Paper Dance: 55 Latino Poets with Virgil Suárez & Leroy Quintana

PANORAMAS

Víctor Hernández Cruz

COFFEE HOUSE PRESS ☕ MINNEAPOLIS

Poems and essays by Victor Hernández Cruz have appeared in: *The World, Sniper Logic, Cupey, Buletin Federico Garcia Lorca, Homeground, The Massachusetts Review, Paper Dance: 55 Latino Poets, Callaloo Magazine, SEE: A Journal of Visual Culture, Language of Life, Poets at Work,* and *Village Voice Literary Supplement*

Coffee House Press is supported in part by a grant provided by the Minnesota State Arts Board, through an appropriation by the Minnesota State Legislature, and in part by a grant from the National Endowment for the Arts; The McKnight Foundation; Lannan Foundation; Jerome Foundation; Target Stores, Dayton's, and Mervyn's by the Dayton Hudson Foundation; General Mills Foundation; St. Paul Companies; Butler Family Foundation; Honeywell Foundation; Star Tribune/Cowles Media Company; James R. Thorpe Foundation; Dain Bosworth Foundation; Pentair, Inc.; Beverly J. and John A. Rollwagen Fund of the Minneapolis Foundation; and many individual donors. To you and our many readers across the country, we send our thanks for your continuing support.

Coffee House Press books are available to the trade through our primary distributor, Consortium Book Sales & Distribution, 1045 Westgate Drive, Saint Paul, MN 55114. For personal orders, catalogs, or other information, write to: Coffee House Press, 27 North 4th Street, Suite 400, Minneapolis, MN 55401.

LIBRARY OF CONGRESS CIP DATA
Cruz, Victor Hernández, 1949-
    Panoramas / Victor Hernández Cruz.
      p. cm.
    Text in English and Spanish.
    ISBN 1-56689-066-7 (alk. paper)
    1.   Puerto Ricans—United States—Poetry.   2. Caribbean Americans—Poetry. 3. Hispanic Americans—Poetry. I. Title
    PS3553.R8P35   1997
    811'.54--dc21   97-16017
                                                       CIP

10 9 8 7 6 5 4 3 2 1

CONTENTS

LETTERS FROM THE ISLAND

PRIMEROS SONIDOS

This gathering of poems
dedicated to a tree and
a rock respectively.
The boulder is located
in the River Borinquen
in the town of Caguas.
The tree is an old man
Ceiba rooted in the valley
between Caguas and Aguas
Buenas visible from the
road 156.

"En estos fastuosos crepúsculos nocturnos puertorriqueños, con tales colores que volverían locos a los pintores barrocos italianos y me vuelven loco a mí cada anochecer, es fácil imaginar cualquier cosa.

Arriba, alrededor, enfrente, el cielo de imposible descripción coloreada por su volubilidad oriental y occidental; abajo, cerca, los arbolados de verde oscuro, recortados como en Botticelli. Y entre ellos y bajo ellos, estas jentes de cuño extraordinario y de una variedad y una orijinalidad tales que parecen vivero de humana animalidad bella.

Y qué plástico y qué química las de tan maravillosas unidades de escena; qué ojos con qué mares dentro, qué bocas con qué nubes en el fondo, qué ritmos con qué tierras en sismo suave sensual."

—Juan Ramón Jiménez
"Isla de la Simpatía"

Home Is Where the Music Is

I was born in a barrio with the name of a Taino fruit: El Guanabano. Located in the central or urban area of the town of Aguas Buenas, Puerto Rico, some 35 minutes from San Juan. The streets of El Guanabano were not yet paved. When it rained, everything became a mess, the downpour created a small river flowing down to the town plaza, the red dirt making the stream appear to be guava juice. Kids would jump outside to play in the torrential tropical showers.

The humidity, the mountain entanglement of lucid bush, spontaneity of trees, and the improvisation of the foliage invented creatures berserk through mating calls of nocturnal coquís—a kind of toad chirping in choral concerto. The native inhabitants of the island were certain that trees were the home of spirits, so they sang poetry to them, asked them in what direction were they walking. To walk the mountains was to encounter the trees as individuals. You could hide from the rain under a Palo de Guayacan; to see from a distant mountain curve a Palo de Roble is to recognize its lavender separating it from the bold green. The fruit of Aguas Buenas is the mamey, a native fruit tree; it has been ripened into ice cream and melted into malt. A tall Palo de Maga points into the clouds while inviting its liquid down. A scattered Palo de Almácigo brushes up arboresque into a Palo de María, assisting in the process of fertilization. A Palo de Higuera hangs round gourds, oval and festive mobiles, worked into bowls by Arawak-speaking hands or into cacique-size maracas to mark the meters of a poem within the arieto. Encountering a Palo de Ceiba is like first communion, sacred to the Tainos; some are hundreds of years old, a huge trunk and its roots can take over a region. Lizards fleeting like electrical charges or suspended motionless for hours awaiting the trajectory of a predestined singular fly. Iguanas, mini crocodiles by the rivers. At night under the mosquito nets the world was a kaleidoscope of sounds, insects, dogs, the dance of trees like layers in the wind. The cucubanos (fireflies) sparkling in the dark, we kids would run after them and palm them right out of the air, put them in clear glass jars, and watch them light up in unison as if we were holding a star in our hands.

All the houses were made of wood; if there was any cement, it was down by the structures that surrounded the plaza where the middle class supposedly dwelled. The windows were small doors that swung open. Many of the houses were elevated off the earth, creating a space underneath, a place where chickens and roosters roamed wild in their persistent flirtation.

Skinny brown legs accompanied packs of mothers heading toward the river to wash clothes. The women used to bang the clothes against the river rocks, hitting the dirt out with pieces of boards as they sang and gossiped, talking, laughing, exchanging information, saying things no man could imagine. We children disappeared into the flora, playing by the eternal contemplation of the cows. Jumping into the river, all of us boys and girls butt-naked, with a giggling and mirth that was recorded by the trees.

The fertile land around us was full of coffee and tobacco, which were the two prominent agricultural crops. We had our own coffee label, "El Jibarito." Coffee was always conducive to conversation, its aroma was the melody of the morning. The campesino custom of the three o'clock cup still maintains its fanatics, unlike the custom of the siesta, the afternoon repose, which is fading in these regions: a rest during the day is bad for production. If they found you horizontal in bed at one-thirty in the afternoon in the northern longitudes, urbanites might christen you lazy, or worse, useless to the economy.

The center of town was full of tobacco workshops known as "chin-chales" in the island vernacular. My grandfather Julio El Bohemio was a well known tabaquero. He was a picturesque character who created a legend for himself as a singer; men were always looking for him to render serenades to the women of their fancy. In the dark of night the silence was broken by guitar strings and harmonic voices in bolero; those songs' lyrics have stayed with me through all metamorphoses of regions and climates. My grandfather would sing "I want the love of dark-skinned women, those bronze ladies of my native earth" to the ears in the heart of the night. They sang Cuban, Mexican, Argentinian, Chilean songs written by composers who were popular poets.

The chin-chales were active places, for the tabaqueros in the Caribbean were notorious for their socialist and anarchist politics, philosophers of the masses, dramatic declaimers of poetry, and, as in the case of my grandfather, singers of the love-romance songs sometimes known as tragedia. Many tabaqueros were rebels and independentistas (those who wanted freedom from Spanish, and North American, possession of the island). Within the context of Caribbean agricultural workers, tabaqueros had a leisurely work pace, freeing their minds for contemplation and aesthetic flight. Coffee pickers, by comparison, had to battle bees all day long, and cane cutters had to chop vigorously under the Caribbean sun. A significant number of tabaqueros went on to become great labor leaders, writers, and historians.

It was within the chin-chales of Aguas Buenas that my imagination first heard poetry declaimed, thrown out loud in coordination with head and hands weaving. I was only a child

13

amidst the tobacco leaves, taken there by my grandfather or my uncle Carlos who used to recite poetic standards like "El Brindis del Bohemio." My uncle continued this tradition of declaiming into the frozen zones of New York's Lower East Side tenements.

Tobacco production employed a good proportion of the town. There were farmers who cultivated the plants in the mountain ranchos, taking meticulous care of them, watching out for tobacco worms and other harmful insects. After the tobacco leaves were harvested, they were allowed to age and dry so that they could acquire their deep aromatic café con leche color. The timing had to be perfect, for while the farmers wanted the leaves to dry, they did not want them to lose all their moisture. Some men dedicated themselves to hauling stacks of bundled tobacco down to the despalilladoras. Despalillar (to remove the center stem from the tobacco leaf) was a task that was accomplished by women; old and young worked side by side, telling stories, reviewing every shadow of public and private life. Nothing escaped their scrutiny, the narratives making the passage of time less monotonous. Once the leaves were done, they were bundled again and sent to all the local chin-chales, where the men rolled them into various styles of cigars. The finished cigars were picked up and taken to massive fábricas for packaging; some of the workers specialized in putting on the ring or little gold wrapper that identified the company and the cigar type. All day they put those little wedding bands on the cigars, keeping an eye out for cigars that appeared to be damaged. It was also within these terminals where the cigars were arranged in their handsome boxes. The whole process took some six months, after which the town went into a slumber.

It is recounted by those who lived during this epoch that the tabaqueros were paid well. They had their golden age. They dressed well: white linen guayaberas, two-tone shoes with white on the top, pra-pra sombreros. The area around the plaza was full of places where you could dance and hear the best orchestras of the day. Cafetin rumor has it that Ramito, Puerto Rico's best-known trovador, spinner of mountain music, once hung out with the tabaqueros of El Guanabano. They went into such a jubilance and frolic of singing and scratching guiro, stomping and dancing that, through beat and vibration, they caused an abandoned and aging wooden house next door to collapse. My grandfather filled the air on Fridays with his white suit and white Panama sombrero. I remember him walking off toward town gleaming clean like white chalk, under the pretext of going to the colmado to buy a pound of café, and vanishing through the hole of a cuatro guitar for two days.

My grandmother Tina must've known him well. When he sculptured that bohemian mischevious grin on his jíbaro face, his features were such that he could have been a campesino from the Río de la Plata region of Argentina, where the tangos that he sang so well were born. Tina Velasquez Ortiz had Africa inside of her, a tall, dark, heavyset woman whose family hailed from the mountain, Jagueyes, which is seen from the center of town, towering like a wall. Situated as we are, not far from the coast, we have a substantial amount of African blood, which in one way or another runs through the community. We are truly criollos and a visual festival. The term *criollo* has meant many different things through different historical periods and regions of Latin America. In some areas it designates a Spaniard born in the New World. To us in Puerto Rico, it has come to mean the mixing of the cultural elements of the Indian, the Spanish, the African—a tripolarity that we recognize in music, dance, physical looks, and cuisine.

My grandmother fell ill with cancer at forty six. In the interior of a small wooden house, I could see her laying in a hammock swinging and singing the pain away, a singing that scaled into a humming that went through the house like a humid vapor. The air had an odor of rubbing alcohol mixed with medicinal plants, a kerosene lantern flickering in her room making shadows dance on a wooden cross. She had eight children, one right after the other plus one that died at birth. She was slowly being eaten by time, dissolving like a chocolate in the sun.

Through a rewind of archived pictures, a Caribbean mulata fries alcapurrias in the combustion of barrio life, green bananas, yautía—part African, part Indian. How did she walk when she was nineteen at the instant my grandfather Julio El Bohemio saw her in the Maria-go-round of plaza coquetry? Did his voice swell in the balada producing spacious gardens of flowers? She drops a handkerchief, they take a stroll into the night, the scent of a mamey tree. Within a glance my mother was born.

My mother, the oldest of the eight children, spent her teenage years helping rear her brothers and sisters. She had her father's gift of singing, and into the despair of the necessities of materialism and the limitations imposed on the female by strong rural machismo, she sang her transcendental boleros. She married young and stayed in the local area, where the effect of the extended family was in force.

In the rural communities, women used to give birth in their own homes with the assistance of a comadrona, or mid-wife. Doña Lola, the comadrona who brought me into the world, came upon the scene of my mother's advanced stages of labor smoking a cigar and flinging herbs toward the sinistral and dextral regions, as if fishing for spirits with hooks so that they can come forward to assist, to align the celestial with the biological process at hand. I was born on a Sunday between five and six in the morning. My mother remembers that Doña Lola made it to seven o'clock mass at the local Catholic church, Los Tres Santos Reyes.

The wooden house where I was born was painted a passion-fruit yellow, adding to the rainbow formed by all the houses on the street. You throw brush with what you got, a blue home next to an orange kiosk, natural wood made gray by age. Gauguin could have come here before going to Tahiti. The color spectrum exhausting itself as El Guanabano housing drops down the sloped street. Time slowly transformed the street into other hues, other textures.

Through a series of chance circumstances, my old house has now been converted into a cafetin—a small community bar and grocery store, a place where men gather to drink, cultivate the art of conversation, tell jokes. Through a further set of coincidences, the cafetin came under the ownership of a cousin of my mother's, Julio Hernández Hernández, who was what I would designate as the popular poet of our town, not a poet of text or literature but a versifier, his poems written in the traditional Spanish forms of coplas and décimas. His compositions approximate the limericks of boleros, the same sentimental, emotional sphere in a language of preconceived formula. Like all popular poets, he had the ability to declaim his verses from memory: going into his cafetin always meant the possibility of a spontaneous outburst of recitation.

The tobacco workshop where my grandfather rolled was directly across the street from where we lived. He worked next to his lifelong friend, Alegría, spicing the rolling of cigars by singing in duo. In the mornings the tabaqueros would put a little money together and hire a reader to come in and read the newspaper, El Imparcial. Other times the tabaqueros would hire a reader to come and read them a chapter of a book a day. It seems that all the tabaqueros in Aguas Buenas were socialists. It was the party of my grandfather Julio El Bohemio, and that's how my grandmother voted too. My mother tells me that when she became eligible to vote, she also voted for the Socialist Party. They were all that way through some kind of popular spirit and not as intellectuals inspired by some economic ideals they had read about. Melodies and people's anarchy arose from a place where the only things affordable sometimes were pride and emotion. Songs entered the leaves to be heard on some future plane within the eventual aroma of smoke.

In the late forties and early fifties, people were speaking of a place called Nujol; it caused a lot of agitation in all sectors of the town. Relatives already up in the northern ledge were sending letters inflating and inflaming imaginations and hopes. There was trouble in paradise. How did that happen in a place so fertile? The greater portion of the rural population was still feeling the effects of many centuries of Spanish exploitation by remote control, medieval economic plans shipped in coffins to the Americas. The conquest still bubbling in the veins. Even objects felt the despair. The pineapple was turning sour in the mountains of sweet music. Where the coffee grew, where the cane was tall, where the aboriginal cigar was grown and rolled, the people said that they saw the devil run, being chased by necessity from the inferno, his very home.

The Puerto Rican tribal-social network helped ease the scarcity of food. Many families heard the call of the yonder, the whispers of the north. People in knots started to untangle and maneuver. Children were left with relatives while parents boarded Eastern Airline propeller planes to the Bronx. Once up there, they stumbled around the English looking for employment, set up a home, and sent for their children.

New York City has been a center for Caribbean immigrants since the late nineteenth century. Exiled Cuban and Puerto Rican revolutionaries established La Sociedad Republicana de Cuba y Puerto Rico in the 1860s to assist in the cause of those on the islands fighting against Spanish colonialism.

Most of the new arrivals from the Antilles moved into the Lower West Side, an area with an established Spanish community. There were Spanish and Argentinian restaurants, bookstores, and a Spanish Cultural Center that continues to exist today. Perhaps many of these Spaniards were Andalusian merchant seamen who came on work visits through the Brooklyn Navy Yard docks, near the areas of Red Hook and Williamsburg, which was also where the first Puerto Rican families settled sometime after the 1900s. Later, after the 1920s, the Puerto Rican community started to sofrito spice the East Harlem area around 100th Street. Tabaqueros constituted a strong force in this first wave of migration.

In El Guanabano, the commotion of cement trucks mixed with the whirlwind of families who were organizing themselves to jump off the edge of the world. It was not the upper classes that had to leave; the bourgeois never leave where they are milking. In proportion to the population of the island, it was one of the most one-dimensional of human exoduses. People were tying boxes like they were pasteles with banana leaves and heading for the iron bird. My mother wanted to know why people kept borrowing our heavy charcoal-heated iron when they were going to fold the clothes and place them in suitcases to become wrinkled again. Puerto Ricans were obsessed with ironing their apparel in those days, and they used a homemade starch to get a crease in a pair of pants that could cut you. Women used to complain that they even had to iron their husband's underwear. This anti-wrinkle mania is something that could be studied. El Guanabano was in a ruckus with public cars taking people to the airport in the mornings and afternoons: tears, hugs, farewells. My grandfather walked through the chaos with a fine grip on his guitar.

My own family jumped on one of those massive waves of island evacuation. The decision was beyond anything I could comprehend. I was busy trying to spilt algarroba seeds in half in a boy's game known as "gallitos." It was our time to go forward into the regions beyond the mountains, from the comforts and hardships of Aguas Buenas to the industry and entertainment, the jungle of concrete and the lights in the hyperborean windows of Manhattan.

I have always been haunted by the strong impression that the first inhalations of cold winter air registered in my childhood nostrils. We migrated from the tropics in the middle of winter. What did we know, coming from one extreme to another, like putting the sun in the freezer. In New York it was snowing. Those who love contrast could satisfy themselves here. We went to the traditional immigrant neighborhood of New York—the Lower East Side, where the tenement buildings towered like magic over us. Had someone poured cement on the mountains, I wondered, recalling all those cement trucks back home. A cold metallic incense permeated the ether, the olfactory of steel, iron, cement, and glass.

English was just a scattering of noise coming out of people's mouths—who could arrange that strange new furniture, where would one sit? Walking slowly, I picked up neighborhood jargon, stoop yap, hallway vocabulary. Out on the streets children exchanged information. Puerto Rican kids had apparently arrived before we did, for I encountered many that were already speaking English, hanging it like fragmented and distorted Cubist paintings. The Lower East Side was full of accents. English waved, leaned, flew, got squashed, shredded, sautéed, made into puree. Italian, Polish, Jewish thoughts danced their own angles into Shakespeare.

On the street where we lived, there was still a Jewish synagogue lingering from the past life of the neighborhood, which was being erased right before our eyes. The local stores were full of things I'd never seen. Jars of sauerkraut, pickles, knishes, winter hats with earflaps that made people look like sputniks, a new empire of gadgetry like that which opened up the eyes of Pinzón, the Spanish explorer. Bubbling it was, flashing, darting, a new vertical comprehension—cars, buses, subways.

The encounter between rural and urban landscape, a debate released through migration, a discussion of spatial tempos, city versus tropical, these are steeped in my conscious-ness and echo through my poetic creations. This for me is the center of metaphor, the sharp contrast that keeps one in northern metros aware of a profound elsewhere. El Guanabano view of the mountains; the Lower East Side view of the Empire State Building. A pendulum swinging between the heat and the cold. The Spanish and English coming together, giving a multiple choice of sounds to select from for objects, experiences, emotions, sensations. For me, writing in straight English or Spanish is always a process of translation—a duality of tongues that opens up a third dimension beyond actual semantics. What comes first in Spanish could come last in English. This same polarization can create problems. It is to the advantage of a writer to be bilingual, but for the general speaker it is best to be anchored in one's native tongue before venturing off into another language. The great Spanish poet Miguel Unamuno said something to the effect that "language is the blood of the spirit." Consequently it is through words that we fulfill our personalities. Without a strong linguistic spine, we could fold into a mush of blah-blah. Because language represents a world, we can see the contradictions that besiege users of the Spanish language in the United States; the world that language is from is not in their presence. Words have lives of their own—they were here before us and they are what we fit into. Experience is the word that passes through the things that we do. Language is a cultural attitude accumulated over the centuries. When I write in Puerto Rican Spanish—the first sounds my body heard and felt when I played in El Guanabano, the ambit of fruits in harmony with boiling manioc—I am writing in a language which has Taino, Arabic-Gypsy-Berber, and African words. In addition, many new vocals were created by the collision of all the energy and diction in the Caribbean.

The Spanish radio programs kept us warm. Flowing from an Emerson radio was Puerto Rican, Cuban, Dominican, Argentinian, Chilean, Mexican music. Being Latin American mestizo is a condition supplied by the crisscrossing of multinations. The cultures go one into another through the common root language, an extended nationalism that includes the entire hemisphere. We danced to the guarachas of Cuba, beat our feet to the rancheras of Mexico, became sad and nostalgic over the boleros of Trio San Jaun.

My father, who was already settled and working in New York when we arrived, had found us a railroad flat on the Lower East Side. It was on the third floor facing the backyard, a steel fire escape hung immediately outside one of the windows. It offered a view uptown toward 14th Street, a Con

Edison electrical plant with pipes systematically dispensing smoke into the sky. Looking to the right, our eyes focused upon the long stretch of brick mountains that made up the edifices of the Avenue D housing projects. We could hear the foghorns of ships on the East River in the mornings as we drank Café Bustelo, getting ready to go out and wrestle with the streets.

In our household there was a constant dialogue, debate, discussion, argument, fight between my mother and father as to when we would get back to Aguas Buenas. Originally the plan was that we would be in New York to work for a period, gather some money, and eventually work our way back home. Every year we would make plans to leave that never got beyond the motions of my mother starting to pack the luggage. Puerto Ricans perfected the art of packaging. They used to fit clothes, personal knickknacks, and even tree bark as snugly as sardines in cans. Rumor has it that back in the fifties, when transportation was bad, Puerto Ricans knew how to get to the airports on public trains.

In the public schools the teachers prohibited the use of Spanish among the recently arrived island children. They would say, "Shusssh-hush, speak in English. It's what's going to get you ahead." Or they'd say, "You're in America now." Looking out the window, we knew we were on the East Side, an aspect of America.

A group of us got in trouble once because of this language problem. We used to have to sing the National Anthem at the beginning of each day. Every time it came to the part "Oh say can you see," most of the students in the class—we were still learning English—heard "José can you see." So we always sang it this way while mumbling something to the two Josés in the room. The teacher—I think her name was Mrs. Straus—was old and had a crooked finger. When she said, "Hey you," and pointed, the person sitting next to the person she meant would always stand up. When she hooked an ear into how we were singing, she separated a group of us—maybe because we had the highest pitch—and made us stay after class. She told us we had to bring our parents in, which was the most embarassing thing. We did, but what was that for? Our parents spoke no English, and there was no one around to translate. So there was Mrs. Straus talking with our island mothers, and our mothers just saying, "Yeah-yeah-yeah." One of them knew how to say the word *right,* going, "Rye-rye." They figured another way to get out of it was by shaking their heads up and down because this would give the impression that they were absorbing information.

As the bricks aged we entered the age of flowers—walking molasses, cha-cha boots, bolero blouses. Mothers found places to make white dresses for their daughters. The youth had inherited the Caribbean spirit of fiesta and carnival and used any excuse to have a party. Over in the Avenue D projects, we'd borrow an apartment and walk the neighborhood fringes inviting every girl we saw. With our portable record players, we formed a bembe anywhere—in the school yard, up on the roof. There we were, sons and daughters of the Antilles throwing pachanga steps, dancing slow to the doo-wop of "The Paragons Meet The Jesters."

The years washed the red mountain dirt from our shoes, but the abyss created by the migration remained like a deep cavity in our wisdom molars, hungry for excavation and filling. Puerto Rican musicians and writers made the journey up north, motivated by reasons of economy and the traditional restlessness of artists. It was an opportunity for the writers to get a bird's-eye view of island politics and culture and their extension in the diaspora.

The music and songs would go back to the island to become part of the cultural panorama of a Caribbean nation. Culture produced on the streets of New York would travel with the people in continuous reverse migration—there is something like an ongoing back-and-forth shift keeping those in the north resupplied with tropical resistance.

Cuban and Puerto Rican musicians met in the clubs and large ballrooms of Manhattan, discussing with each other new levels of rhythms and polyrhythms. On 110th Street at the now-defunct Park Palace Ballroom the music was on fire way before it traveled downtown to the famous Palladium. I was too young in the early fifties to make it to these dramas of island life in the States. It was like fiestas patronales indoors. I watched my uncle Juan and my aunt Chela get glazed up with those shoes that used to look like glass to go to these mambo groves. With their friends they would form balls to take the subway together to 53rd Street, where the Palladium was. They would all get back late, couples kissing all over the hallways, leaning against brass mailboxes, then taking off their shoes to walk up the marble stairs. In the mornings when I was sent out to get bread for the coffee, I could smell the scent of gardenia perfume lingering in the hallway.

The music of the guitar and the music of the drum came together in the ears and hearts of a bilingual generation bred in the States. Everything was jumping with Symphony Sid in the city; he had a late-night radio program playing the New York-based Cuban and Puerto Rican music. (It wasn't called salsa then, that can came later.) A dance called the pachanga, which featured some vicious foot stomping, was knocking buildings down. My generation developed a boogaloo with Latin rhythms and English lyrics. Dancers started jumping all around the floor. Building roofs were stretched with conga drum hide, and something was playing them.

On a clear summer night of my youth, I was trying to search for some sleep, staring from a third-floor window at the moon, which seemed to be falling into one of the pipes of the Con Edison plant. There was too much energy elevating up. Out on the street a group was drumming an African beat through which they wove a Spanish Gypsy canto hondo. Goya and Velázquez paintings were melting into Bantu shrines, someone was shaking native maracas into the brick Bohíos. As I looked down toward the sound, it appeared like a gathering of agricultural tribes in a fertility fest—Hindu Gypsies, Andalusians, Asturians, Arabs, Congolese, nomadic Berber shepherds. It was such a kaleidoscope that I decided to paint the fire escape gold. By morning it was dry and the drums had turned to strings. The troubadors were praising a lady, studying her walk, as they measured the meter of the verse. The morning light brought images out of the haze.

I remembered then, sitting in the sunshine out on the fire escape, the songs of my grandfather Julio El Bohemio, the proclaimer of poems around the old chin-chal of tobacco in the town of my childhood. The mountain, Jagueyes, blocked out the projects. Sitting upon the golden mineral, I got the urge to write, to tell a story as if from a balcony, use the juices of a guanavana for ink. I knew I would some day go back with words, searching for the past in the future. I knew my body was right, right where it was. With Hugh Masekela, I second the emotion expressed by his album "Home Is Where the Music Is."

THE AGE OF SEA SHELLS REVISITED

The Lower East Side of Manhattan

By the East River
of Manhattan Island
Where once the Iroquois
canoed in style—
A clear liquid
caressing another name
for rock,
Now the jumping
Stretch of Avenue D
housing projects
Where Ricans and Afros
Johnny Pacheco / Wilson Pickett
The portable radio night—
Across the Domino sugar
Neon lights of the Brooklyn shore

Window carnival of
megalopolis lights
From Houston Street
Twenty kids take off
On summer bikes
Across the Williamsburg
Bridge
Their hair flying
With bodega bean protein
Below the working class
jumping like frogs—
Parrots with new raincoats
swinging canes of bamboo
Like third legs

Down diddy-bop 6th Street
of the roaring Dragons
Strollers of cool flow

When winter comes they fly
In capes down Delancey
Pass the bites of pastrami
Sandwiches in Katz's
Marching through red bricks
aglow dragging hind leg
Swinging arms
Defying in simalcas

Hebrew prayers inside
metallic containers
Rolled into walls
Tenement relic
Roofs of pigeon airports

Horse-driven carts
arrive with the morning
Slicing through venetian
blinds
Along with a Polish English
Barking peaches and melons
Later the ice man a-cometh
Selling his hard water
cut into blocks
The afternoon a metallic
slide intercourses buildings
Which start to swallow
coals down their basement
Mouths.

Where did the mountains go
The immigrants ask
The place where houses
and objects went back
Into history which guided
Them into nature

Entering the roots of plants
The molasses of fruit
To become eternal again,
Now the plaster of Paris
Are the ears of the walls
The first utterances in Spanish
Recall what was left behind.

People kept arriving
as the cane fields dried
Flying bushes from another
planet
Which had a pineapple for
a moon
Vegetables and tree bark
popping out of luggage
The singers of lament
into the soul of Jacob Riis
Where the prayers Santa Maria
Through remaining fibers
of the Torah
Eldridge Street lelolai
A Spanish never before seen
Inside gypsies.
Once Cordova the cabala

Haberdasheries of Orchard Street
Hecklers riddling bargains
Like in gone bazaars of
Some Warsaw ghetto.

Upward into the economy
Migration continues—
Out of the workers' quarters
Pieces of accents
On the ascending escalator.

The red Avenue B bus
disappearing down the
Needle holes of the garment
factories—
The drain of a city
The final sewers
Where the waste became antique
The icy winds
Of the river's edge
Stinging lower Broadway
As hot dogs
Sauerkraut and all
Gush down the pipes
of Canal

After Forsyth Park
is the beginning of Italy
Florence inside Mott
Street windows—
Palermo eyes of Angie
Flipping the big

hole of a 45 record
The Duprees dusting
Like white sugar onto
Fluffed dough—
Crisscrossing
The fire escapes
To arrive at Lourdes'
railroad flat
With knishes
she threw next to
Red beans.

Broome Street Hasidics
with Martian fur hats
With those ultimatum brims
Puerto Ricans supporting
pra-pras
Atop faces with features
Thrown out of some bag
Of universal race stew—
Mississippi rural slang
With Avenue D park view
All in exile from broken
Souths
The horses the cows the
chickens
The daisies of the rural
road
All past tense in the urbanity
that remembers
The pace of mountains
The moods of the fields.

From the guayaba bushels
outside of a town
With an Arawak name
I hear the flute shells
With the I that saw
Andalusian boats
Wash up on the beach
To distribute Moorish
eyes.

The Lower East Side
was faster than the speed
Of light
A tornado of bricks
and fire escapes
In which you had to grab
on to something or take
Off with the wayward winds—

The proletariat stoop voices
Took off like Spauldine
rubber balls
Hit by blue broomsticks
on 12th Street—
Wintertime summertime
Seasons of hallways and roofs
Between pachanga and doo-wop
A generation left
The screaming streets of
passage
Gone from the temporary
station of desire and disaster

I knew Anthony
and Carmen
Butchy
Little Man
Eddie
Andrew
Tiny
Pichon
Vigo
Wandy
Juanito
Where are they?
The windows sucked them up
The pavement had mouths that
ate them
Urban vanishment
Illusion
I too
Henry Roth
"Call It Sleep."

Invisibility O

Planets of air
Angels and music
Between us all
Molecules screwing
Humidity
Through bubbly globes
Pink and hazy
See through ice teeth
Chewing up the wind—
Transparent gobs of manure
Synchronized with space waves—
Pork dog stench shapes
Monstrously created by
Crumbled aspirations.
Anteaters' coitus with
Mountain swine in thought—
Fluid snakes the size of ships
Moving between the cities dressed
In ultraviolet fog
Insane moans moving through
Hallways of clouds
Where fly holy spirit birds
Who eat electric umbilical
Wires making sounds
Which are plugged into
The air surround
Melting vagabundo entities
Vacationing in matter
Monstrous images
Chunking up atmosphere

Earth contaminated
By objectional distance
Made of air and wind
Perfumed by gardens of
olfactory fumes
Breaths of sulfuric gases
Passages of murky soup
Mist of carbon dioxide
On wings of bats
Liturgy of vampires' lust
Sheets of memory traveling
Endless planks
Alchemy: gooey-looking
Caterpillars fly away
As flowers
Juices of emotion making
Lightning sounds from Mars
Luciferian radiation beaming down
From Venus
Firing up vicinity and distance
Primeval space where tobacco
Was imagination rolling
The ringing of a cloudy phone
Over
Mountains whose dress is a
Gown of clear crystals
A sky orchestra playing
Cavernous corners of limestone
Shingalin of heavenly echoes
An island of sound ovals
Entering antennas
Vengeful skeletons splicing

out of air pockets
Doors made of aroma
Azucena, la siciliana,
Spread of night
Like campana of magic carpets
Banana leaves floating
On four primal colors
Of sun going through rain
Nectar left by macaws
Who have been perched
On café branches
Bees orbit the concert
Of coffee cups brewed
The sky a page full of
Clouds for all that is
Apparent
Above the crossroads
of the faithful pupils

Hot Thought

The idea that something called
the greenhouse effect is at work
Enhances when you Caribbean encompose—
Would it get hotter in the valley
of Caguas just for an instant
of thought calderón—
Or southerly more yet Coamo
Where they say it never rains
Even ice in the freezer
loses its stance.

Is it going to get hotter
Than a mid-October Ponce
Afternoon?

Will we reach the point
where our flesh tenderizes
And slowly cooks in the air—
Will we see our skin
Slide off our bones
As we walk across the plaza
Making a last attempt to
get to the ice cream vendor—
Before they both melt.

The Face Without Makeup

Pictograph this:
If we awoke one day
Let's say tomorrow
And all the oceans
Were dried up—
Every last drop
You can go out
And walk on the
Beds of the oceans
Stare out into the
Swirls of new landscape
The whole visual
For eye and telescope
Binoculars catch
The sight of a trillion
Tons of sea creatures
Doing the jerk—
Octopus and whale
Shark and sardine
Down there sunbathing
Post'd as if in a Fish
Market—
Then you'd see that
The Earth is not round,
It is more like clay
Fashioned by Salvador Dalí.

It's Miller Time

I work for the CIA
They pay me with cocaine
and white Miami sports
Jackets
Free tickets to San Juan
Where I make contact
with a certain
Official at the Chase
Manhattan Bank

My contact, a guy named
Pete, asks if I know other
dialects of Spanish
"Can you sound Salvadoran"
They give me pamphlets
along with pornographic mags
They got their hands in the
backdoors of warehouses
If I want a stereo or a CD
That if a VCR
They could bring it all
at half price
Tickets to rock and roll
concerts
Where they drug the people
with lights.

The last assignment
I had was to contact
the PR division

Of a beer company—
Because for u.s. "Hispanics"
it was Miller Time
I contacted the brewery
A certain Miguel Gone-say-less
Invited me to lunch
That to meet him at La Fuente
Plush frijoles
Girls in peasant blouses
serving—
Low-key mariachi birdly
Community program directors
dining their secretaries
Big ol' bubble of tie knots.
At a back table there he
was
Drinking Dos Equis
and cracklin' tortilla chips
With him was a Camden, New Jersey,
Cuban who was going through
Town en route to Los Angeles
The lunch was on them—
Señor Gone-say-less
Had credit cards thickly
He had more plastic than Woolworth's.

They mentioned that the
beer company wanted to sponsor
Salsa dances within the community
Bring in the top commercial
orchestras
. . . and that while this dance was

Going on they wanted to pass
a petition against u.s. involvement
in Central America—
They demonstrated the form of some
organization they invented
Latinos Against Intervention
The petition had space for
the name and address of the
signers
A great list to have and share
among all government agencies.

They gave me a bag with three
thousand dollars in it—
It was my responsibility to
organize the petition circulation.
The Cuban guy tapped me on the
shoulder and said:
"Don't have any of the mixed drinks.
The bartenders at the dance are
working for us. The chemical people
are experimenting the effects of
a new liquid. Just drink the beer."

The festive event was smashing
people were stuffed into a ballroom
The band smoked
The beer company gave out caps
Ladies dressed like Zsa Zsa Gabor
Romeos thrown back propped for image
Circling the ice of their margaritas—
A full moon gleamed into downtown.

Next week the CIA
is flying me back to the
Caribbean
where I will assist in staging
One of the strangest events in
world history,
According to the description we
are going to pull off a mock
Rising of land from beneath
the Caribbean
Which the media will quickly
identify with Atlantis—
Circular buildings made of crystals
are being constructed in Texas
They will be part of the
Espectáculo
Which will have the planet
spellbound
Simultaneous with this event
the Marines will invade the
Countries of Nicaragua and
El Salvador from bases in Puerto Rico.

It will be a month of salsa fests
in San Francisco
An astounding mystical event off
Bimini
The price of cocaine coming through
Miami will drop
Everybody stunned party and
celestial
Glittering frozen and drunk

Circuits jammed with junk and
Information

In a daze of rapid commercial
flight
Colonialism and business
Mark their 500th anniversary
the world is free
It's Miller Time.

Signed: Double Agent El Lagarto

Islandis

This is the taste of the
Guavas of Hesperides
That converted a sabor
Of eyes on loan from the sun.

Was the Carib isles
The ink in the plume
Of Plato—
In the philosopher's mind
A sandy curve of coast
Stretching into red soil
And sky out into the lamps
Of the Gods.

Mayagüez plain Maya
Before the Castilian Quez—
Yabucoa the town's name is
Singing
A stepping-stone to Atlantis—

Spectacular ships entered
The domain of Humacao
Guided by red corals
And the incense of gold
Navigational songs of the nymphs
Spiraling out of seashells.

Were the coquís ten times
Louder in ages remote
Could they have been

The singing notes
That drove Homer's sailors mad.

Did someone speak of Anacaona's
Hairdo of braids weaved
With gardenias
Tainas threaded live cucubanos
Through their tresses
Sparkling lights through
The nights parallel to Hellenic
Theater girls dancing
In some Roman antiquity of
Cordova—

Let us bow our heads
In silence
Pushed back to the twilight
Of ideas
And with the next Venusian
Light to telegram into
Manatí
Declare ourselves
The kings and queens
Of Poseidon
Wearing crowns of
Bird gone feathers.

Mesa Blanca

If I were writing on rock,
It would be the wind of the year
That caressing me will make
Me aware of the shadows on
A distant stone—
That signifies an eclipse
On some unseen distant roof,
From where in the form of
A kite a diamond leaves for heaven.

It would be that sound that I would
Make into a face,
Present it at the banquet of those
Who came lost on the boats
Punctuate on key
A coco-net of cybernetic eyes
Transmitting from the beach.

The sea a rush of mists,
Christ carrying the cross of Castile
Soldiers laundering heads of crushed guava
Have popped out of there
Salty like bacalao which here has been
Fricasseed with calabaza,
So we have to church the word
Mestizo
Half and Half—
So that textbooks claiming total
Taino vanishment
Should four pages later erase

The word *Mestizo*,
With the same mouth they say we are,
Was Webster wasting his time:
"mes-ti-zo [Sp, fr. *mestizo*, mixed, fr. LL *mixticius*]
a person of mixed blood; *specif:* a person of mixed
European and American Indian ancestry."

The sensational things coming together,
Of the Arawak-Taino
The only thing that remains is
What is not gone:
The looks,
The gestures,
The thoughts,
The dreams,
The intuitions,
The memories,
The names of fruits,
Rivers,
The names of towns,
Vegetables,
Certain fish,
The gourd making music
In the mountain,
The maraca making feet
Areyto dance,
And this cigar between my fingers.
More than half is the ground itself
The rock in my hands was in Arecibo's palm.
This is not to disagree with the
Anthropologists of text
But merely to reaffirm what they mean
When they don't say.

This paper which was a tree
Is crying for its leaves
That's the route of your mind
To dance its branches,
For that canopy red flower
Of the Antilles,
So high up in air spirit,
Flowing right through that bark,
A water shaft,
A city of bamboos
Liquefied fructus,
Humid swamp for that
Night frog,
To sing without rest
Till the roosters brush their
Beaks with the first
Arriving morning light.

The joyful noise of the night
What might be coming from lips,
Or the rubbing of legs
The full harmonic tropical berserk
Begging for love
In abundance
Not one thousand
But one thousand and one
Lights of cucubanos,
Morse-coding lovers,
That come down,
Meow not now
Of the cats—

For that's the flavor,
Within the opening of the
Two mountains,
A glance following the
River
That goes to fish its memories,
Scratched one next to the other
Like the grooves of shells,

To think that no one believes
We are here.
The past in the smoke of the cigar,
Bringing the future in-formation.

*

If a kiss left the mental dimension,
Entering the bone of dance hall,
My ears will reclaim the sound
Of your intended love.

Mostly it would be lost.
Both the poetry and the music
But to this side of things only,
'Cause flashing in the joy
Is the lord of the station,
So immediate as to almost
Be your tongue,
The salivic pointed,
When it truths together,
That moment when decisions are over,
And the motion is the only thought

Accomplished I hear the buttons
Slipping through the grooves of
Your fingertips
Out through the ether of the
Hole slice,
Now the back opens
As onto a land
Curving into a cave,
Most a moist is there—
That even fries lips
Which when the language dissolves
Gets hot enough to eat.
And it is always like this.
And it is only like this.
Ah Ha.

*

You were definite perfume
Aroma of incense that became voice,
Waving pink and blue plastic curtains,
Designs of Greek pillars
Contrasting with a wooden mountain house,
You left in criollo curls
And in the little tails of a glance—
I saw you in a Ford Granada
A silver metal moving like a star
Through the Catalan balconies—
You left in March
Through a rain forest
And came out in Ponce
Inside little bottles of water.

Children in the playa
Rubbing them with their coconut palms—
Floated you out as a giant head
Over the plena tambourines
The Moorish turban of Mahoma
Folding onto the rhythms—
Made on the backs of goats—
Riding them from the Caribbean
To the Atlantic
The crescent of the isle—
Descending through Sumidero
Once again the fragrance—
It became sound in the plaza
That swayed hamacas
Between the backstairs of the eye
And the windows of the nose—
Producing the melodies of an image—
Evidently.

*

The caciques were descendants of hydrogen
The sun hung upon their chest
Candles near the Indian Head
Simaron rockets
They passed singing through
Maví trees and rock—
They migrate with the blood
And filter through bricks
Going toward feathers—
In the frozen ice a gold head
Ring upon a finger calls

And the water boils as if
For tea star anise—
When the prayer takes cadence
Someone's hands circles in the
Rising heat
Elevating from the intestines
A stream
Canoes in fierce paddle
Passing the throat
Broadcasting splinters of words
Like a prairie fire
En route to ignite the Crown.

*

A brush of airs full of words—
Ink on limestone marble—
The house itself is a poem,
Enter through the word: See
Shadows and rhythmic stone.
Sara churns 2,000 pieces of silk,
Passports for sailors,
Shepherd streams in the desert,
A caravana of gold tooth wagons,
Long skirts and sharp eyes.
A string vibes in the air
The ear that heard the doors
Of the Cathedral of Burgos open:
Arco de Santa María—
El Cid and his sword
Pointed on the parchment—
Riding the sweet eyes of a little girl

Into the stare of macabre machos
Thirsty for blood.
Peace and rage
The picture brings memory to its knees.
The stroll of a scroll pulled
From the pocket of a Cataluña Street.
In the presence of the past—
Coming back to wonder
How a fresh of air
Can come and bow amongst us—
In the humid Antillean—
From dream to terror:
From Bohíos to apartments
From cathedral to mosque
Words ironed into stone.

The Castilians were coming
Out of the mouth of a volcano
Falling as ash unto red dirt.
Orocovis navel earthenware—
Artisans of finger palms
Had designs for each fruit taste
It is that subtle of a music
What silence for cadence split
Coffee people to enter you
Tobacco people to enter you
Sugar cane to enter you.
Corozo palms supply the material
For the black asabache
The space between stars
To enroll your finger
Vegetable craft

Working bones
Placing mother-of-pearl
Like light into the seeds
Three years before Columbus
The future spoke
The mouth of Volcanos:
Ashes.

*

Sprinkled all over the distance
Was the gossip that I'd been
Seen inside of a can
Thrown on the side of a road
Leading toward the songs of Ramito—
With a straw hat of fine stitching
At the same moment that
I was observing
A double-nothing
Lock a game of dominos
Closer down to the plaza
In the lime of El Zaragoza—
With the Ivory locked in hands
The matter was this—
What began with double sixes
Went into six trios
That ended in two fours—
Which was all the calculus
Don Felo needed to know
It was all going toward nothing—
So he held on to the empty frames
The counting fell precisely

'Cause outside a woman was calling
A girl named Cucha—
A man who knew twice the nothing
Rang: "That's the one."
When a player slammed down
One with four
To which the next one
Put four with blank—
Don Felo, who held the chucha
As Cucha walked by,
He saw the beginning of the end
Since everyone else had shot
Their blanks—
That's how it was possible
To highlight the night
Without leaving the can
Iluminiam of literature.
That's how the rumor spread
Into the arena
Of popular especulación.

That's why even when it's nothing
La chucha is everything.

*

What is the melody in the mountains,
Tubors imagining deep in dirt,
Used to be chanted rosaries
A cadence emerging out of wood,
Down ravine circling region
Eating the wide silence—

In trance with the rosary beads
A medieval gloss,
They lived in María's womb.

The coast what it got—
Rhythms and waves—
Palms clapping awake perfume
Humid women in plaza dance
Tongues out of mouth
At the men who jump in the shadows
Panama hats transmitting
Toward the radar
Of the waist.

Cucaracachas in the chickens dance
The roosters bebop.

Heat that sweat is the ink
A calor in Spanish that
The Church starts to run
Down Avenida Piel de Canela.

Hot waters rising through the
Songs of minerals
As mountain and coast
Morel Campos danza—
Antique contraband bones,
Flesh of bamboo walking
Senegal the Force Feet
of the mountain trovador
Rhythm golden bird
Inventing itself on the
Spot.

A disjoint of bone
Like yoga
The Rig Veda becomes
Foot and step—
From Guayama the priest
Ferment of herbs
Frog breath
Lizard tail
Opticals of owls
And all the fires there are.

What choice do you have:
Might as well jump toward
land like seed
Tongue in moisture
With green mountain light
And coastal curves—
To lick the invisible
Generations.

PANORAMAS

"Paisaje que no pasa nunca:
cierro los ojos y lo veo."

—Xavier Villaurrutia

The flora
Looked like books shelved
Out on the horizon and available.

Jobos of guanavana poetry,
Madrigals of papaya,
Haikus of lime
In perfect time
Through abundant roots
Of passion fruits—
Next to breadfruit encyclopedias—
Greeting the air
Before it lectures
Those who chance through window
A lustful invitation—
Moisture yellowing pages—
Verbal white birds flapping
Into the chapters.
Beaks that verse the prose.
The camp position invaded
By insects—
Biting the history that lurks
In caverns
Known to the reptiles of research,
And written in the Sunrise of roosters.

The river flowing through the sound: Guaraguao
Before the buildings rose,
A mouth singing vegetables
The coast as always
Receiving fire power,
The turn of the screw,
A screw in the fruit,
A mouth changing with the taste,
Where the sweetness turns sour.

Now the current is flowing without the view.
A past tense grows in the absent terrain.
As if language lived without our mouths to express it,
Little bottles of paint for the brush of rhythms.

Tiempo chasing tempos,
A string takes a siesta
Inside a maraca gourd,
Geo-swing instrumental trade,
The music of history
Below and above swords and cannons
The truth of the melody guarachin.

Walking from Africa
Camel of olive eyes,
A finger plays its neck,
A charm that can walk through
A palace displacing Roses.
Infinity of stars falling
Running through Yoruba sandglass
A Northern impulsion
Palm oil across metallic wire.

The Rock of Gibraltar motions
To write ballads around the
Belly button of Granada maidens,
The guitar a replica of her waist,
Castanets rain up into the
Stars that come out at day.

From the caves songs flying
Out like bats,
Language like sauce drumming
The streets.
Lips that visual.
Eyes that speak.
Painters mandala the eyes
Of Magdalena,
The father of Christ
A geometric sensation
Invisible like the love affair
With María.

Across vast liquid—
Taino classics
Filtering counsel out of seashells.
Tapping entities asleep in trees,
Inside rocks.
Gold and feathers
Brushing the guiros,
As they guide the legs
Through continental-island shifts,
Give us our daily cassava,
A thought of sky
Where the books are birds,
Inventing impressionism.

Messengers from the Sun
Drinking pineapple wine,
Agueybaná knew by heart
Memory 300 songs
And the names of his thirteen wives,
His forehead the wood
For ultraviolet solar etching.

The stomach of turtles
Adorn the pots,
The power of the wind
A drawing on your chest.

Skin music
Migrating to the point
Of a shoe
Tito Puente shifts
Dividing the edge of a razor in half,
Like Muhammad did the moon.

Landing into squares and rectangles
The bronze incarnation,
The wings of history
In a glance
That will give birth
To travel once again
The caterpillar makes itself a dress.

What is in the night for you,
Pure heavenly China gardenia scream,
Sideways the machete a reflecting mirror,
As so sharp and astute the flower pictures,
Molasses: Cuts you in half.

Collapsing like moths into light,
The skirts lifting with the eyelid,
Avocados falling ass first,
Can you imagine a coconut
Lands smack into a mamey,
It's the cause of the night,
What is in the water bowl
Creating electrical flashes,
Possession moving the whole sense,
Through this forest of legs walking in events,
Flickering like a want,
Wondering what is that hanging in the
Trees, bananas or fish?

And just when you are really tranquil
The shadow of a fragrance crawls up the wrist,
The Antillean curve melody,
A production of dresses
The offspring of 19th-century agriculture,
Pre-industrial statues chewing fruit divine,
When they made a festival out of barbwire soup:
And survived—
How delightful can misery be
When forgotten?
Holding the breath of a hurricane
Those who survived are happy
With their scars.

Thunder wakes you up
To notice a lion in the room,
Reach for the machete in the mirror,
The beast's eyes are made of roses,
A wink and you're dead,
Nostalgia of frying yucca,
A white hat eating shades of green,
Taking the head off,
Palms dancing above tambourines,
Clearing
The retina of an owl
Throwing fire into the dark pages
That turn, turning the sky.

What disappeared appears,
It never left,
Aligning rocks to the sun,
Threw my ear to the ground
Listening to the footsteps of
Turtles that passed
A millennium ago.

Ponce mulata waist that
Runs the waves,
Writing out of see,
Marking
With the cosmic point of feet,
The shoulders,
The tongue,
Navigating
A caligrafía of the cavernous night,
Pictographs edging off the stone,

A penmanship coming out of the bay
Like a moon glow.

Don't ever sleep again.

The horizontal song disappears into a
Cane of heavens,
Walking up a cement and cal
Frosting sheets of zinc.
Ears are fingers
The night transmitting
The mountain pueblo
Gathering speed
Forming into a rock
Inventing the commercial jumps
The economic leaps
A cod fritter for two cents
Frozen in recollection.
There are those who well
Have deceived themselves
Splashly out of awareness
Into a dim of shadows
That the senses barely
Transport as they march
To the ongoing church
Satana never lacks friends,
It's in the swiftness of their walk,
It's in how fast their faces came
And have gone,
In locomotion losing
The capacity to designate
A drum into stories,
Well-spoken momentos
A voice into a tale
To send charm
Where there is a drought of love.

Sharp knives that sting the air
To death
Noise into the tenderest ears
That will melody to the next
Generation,
Each time the same persons
Start the same Journey
As if in an endless standing still.

Your thought can leave from
The corners of the tobacco
Café Molased street
And pierce the length of the planets.
If at least one staff
Steps on its note:
Celebrate
'Cause those two ears come together
To make the shape of a heart
Listening
Above the rain forest.

Ambitious rains of moist September
The petal and the thorn bathing,
Mammoth love flowers,
Orchids
Covering with a fingernail the sky,
Diminishing trees and mountains,
Breaking into smaller pieces
Feeding the mouth of a guitar,
Strings of vines,
A neolithic chant
Manitas de Platas
Caves.

Argologo of bones
Skull thunder
Maria Clay
Play India
Rivers gone to air,
A moon of glass
Reflections
Guayaba tune taste
Flower flight
Rhythm sight.

Hands which were eyes,
In the wrist of maracas,
A necklace was a dress,
The embroidery of Andalusia
Captured sound of castanets,
Landscape opened like a fan
Encouraging rivers of tears.

Love which was before the
Bodies were born,
Breaking in the waves,
Having not yet arrived
To this mountain isolation.

Out in the maze in the minerals,
In the trees that will become beats,
The song will finally come to you
In a gulp of corn,
Birds' (Guaraguao) view
Of some cathedral mountain inside.
Steeples made of azucenas
Garza wings white:
Let it rain.
Monet brushing the breasts of Cayey.

*

Wait till you see Venus on her knees.
You will forgive the tongue-lashing
As nothing,
A kiss into the firmament
Between papaya and jobos
Light beams of the higuera moon
Each mile is a thrown hip
Till you exact the Dipper,
Charging seeds in the waist,
The voltage of a buckle.

The watts of Quike y Tomas
Explains the absence,

If it left one day,
Desire circles back
Till once again you are
A plaza glance.

*

Red ochre on your ass—
In the mountains
Gods whose names
Have been forgotten
Or mispronounced in Castilian.
Letters don't sound like trees
Voices barking bark
Lip to lip
Ceiba landwhich.

*

Conversation reaching the timing
When at precision: Two are gone.
A plumage of eyes begins:
Her hands lifting a white cloud
The shape of a calabaza,
In the limestone of caves
Naked in banana leaves,
With all the shells
That survived the Ice Age,
Putting into the same maracas
Seeds,
A jumping toad on her feet
A word to think of is: *Pana-Rana.*

Fertility locked in rock.
You hear the river you cannot see.
Darker than closed eyes
In black night.

Succumb.
Without question:
Serve to be served.

*

The song is horizontal
For at least a day or two.
It has its length
Walking up a cane
Of years held by mahogany
Paws
The fan of ether
That used to mold stone.

Faces speed against place,
In a hurry through the Panorama
Must be Satanas coming back
From doing one of his.

Are those the people who killed
Christ in the church / again.
Its capacity to nerves:
A pitch of erotica
Covered with clouds,
Tied in moño knots.
Swampy frogs jumping
The air of knives.

Huh, there's trouble in paradise
A drought of love
Stings the air.

This rush is in exile here.
I got a stress that won't translate.

In generations away
Each time the same
Journey
As if in an endless standing still.

The song has such length that
Soon you won't be in it.
The view we see
Belonged to another time
Other people upon it Mapayed.

And that if you heard it yet:
Right there build a shrine
'Cause if at least one staff
Steps on the note
The large night drops
Into the paint of Campeche.

*

No one here,
But me and the mountains.
The blue language
The soil wind,
Green bites.

Staring at a mountain
Till it grew a mouth to kiss,
Verdal suck.

*

Frozen flowers,
Dance when lightning hits.
On fire all the way to the water,
All flowers are temptation.
All dresses are made of flowers
All trees are tempted to fly
Into the sky,
A fragrance of control
Soils them in root.
One night a red angel
Dances the dandies flute,
Flowers reach coconut juice
To drink.
The outlet found:
They say, ah, keep it there
Keep it there
Keep it there.

*

Wet black hair
When light tickles
The entrails of the night.
The flame receives a cool
Breeze from the maze.

Where are the singers from,
Where are the trumpeters going,
What are the drummers doing?

One member of the band disappears.
In the plaza the dance continues,
The crowd,
The salsa.
Gone:
The saddle, the trumpet
And the horse.

That's 'cause everyone was staring
At the eclipse—
When closer by
There was a movement
Behind the lid of her eyes.

Conjunctures of the Caribbean,
The foot to the ankle in the sand,
Pumping salt out to the air,
Coconut is an innocent bystander
Which will assist in any shamelessness.
Now see how it slips
Now see how it shines,
After the trumpet
Came the timbales
Creating such a friction,
That had it not been for the rain,
The firemen would have arrived.

*

The index finger tracing turtle bellies,
Play clay sway pot in hut
For when the senses were coming to gone,
An imitation of a dream with juice,
That special cup of measuring moon,
Ceramic pottery miles below
The Christian skulls.

Flowers fruits vegetables
Not far a city kingdom arising—
The slaves and masters
Trying to live another game.

Pirates' ships on coastal riffs
Deeper yet loose mountaineers
Original copper
Spanish tramps
Painting Ollers olla
A new smell
With the pitirre birds
Lacing above the frame.

Other plains
Horsing through/
What can we say
How the root of the drum
Went like a white
Bird—
Dancing in coastal
Variations—

Pachangalandia
Of each and every
Curve of street.

Each place is hot
Each place is tough.
All plates have spice.

Caravan cumbia that left
Down Vallanata Bahía,
Planning plenas that
Merengue inside—
If each one of those
Movements
You strip to the bone—
Bomba
Cumbia
Rumba
Flamenco
Plena
Illuminating a cast of hips
In simalcas
A straw hat bopping through
White cement.

Art is motion standing still—
The furnace burning
The sparks of the sacrifice
Proceeding
Through the carnival
Fiestives.

History can do what it does,
Fire burns everywhere.

*

I dreamt that there were horses
Galloping upside down in the caves,
Stomping the guts of the mountains—
As the people stared into the blue
Wondering where all the thunder
Was coming from.

The same when the mare is in heat—
Get out of the way,
For horses have been known
To break a town to pieces,
Back when everything was wood.

Let a mare walk by at night,
Nightmare—
The stallion charges—
As if a force jumping
Out of hell.

*

There is a seashell
Coming through the air,
Creating a hiss that
Is now registering
in the candles of Brazil.

The earth will feel
The pulse of the wind
And a roar—
As if the ocean stood
Up in vertical fright.

People: Headaches
The radio telescopes
Can't find the frequency.

A seashell of beautiful
Surface whirlpool etchings.
Enclosing the ocean ballet.

Into eternity goes a grain
Of sand
All that the earth is
Inside a single groove
Of the shell.

*

Two times I saw you,
Two times dressed different you were,
So I called you once Anise,
And the second time Cocoa.

The first address you gave me
Was wrong,
Said you lived by the ocean,
Now you put it in the sierras,
Lost in the electric trees.

Both times it was you,
With different faces.
So nice you were made twice.
Choosing from those mountain ghosts,
Centuries by a flowing river,
Hiding from the historical process.
A love before words to speak
Before soil and lips,
A darkness of light speaking,
A mustache picking up the thunder,
Choosing the horizon flavor.

Now I wait for you to turn your face,
Before I call out your name,
Could be reptiles and horses
Climbing up your head.
Whatever
The changing moods of the
Lizard skin moon.
When we dance
Each turn a different mask.
A black berry,
The cinnamon bark,
An olive branch,
The mineral copper,
The falcon of the Berbers,
A Río Platense shine,
Your face inspiring
Local sonneteers/decimeros
It is within the crazy flora
Up all night taking pictures
With an owl

For the sun to develop them
In daylight.
The four faces took one
Picture Together.
Look now:
The salamander's face.

Some fish in reefs
Are like wet flowers.
Some went to give
The name of a fruit
To a neighborhood,
That's the barrio
Where I was born,
An Arawak fructification:
El Guanabano
Where I first saw
A version of you.
All around us
Whispering in rivers
And disguised as vegetation,
The pain of our language,
It knows the place we are,
But not who is speaking.

*

There is a printing
In the chance slaps and rustlings
Of the leaves.
Penmanship blowing in the wind.

Breeze that has traveled from afar,
Dipped ink in coastal salt,
Then went perfuming through
Mountains and valleys,
To circle a papaya,
Finally to gust through an open
Window
Where a body asleep
Sensates the momentary rush
The indoors of a Karmen,
Nothing could be fresher,
The sky avails itself in the house,
An air of desire,
A remembrance of
The flowered illusion,
Pano-ramas.

Comprehending the arrangement
Between the ingredients and the taste,
A going without knowing
Into each other
Of part and part
The conversation of silence
Timing of duality precise
As if you came into a forest
And turned into a leaf

There is no salvation
For the burning invisible
A red statue
Dressed in a blue gown
Dripping out of a thought.

Accept what is walking
Graceful sky
Her hands lifting a white cloud

Fingers rolling out of two palms
Held up toward the three tree palms
Whence the division jumps into
The same maraca
Frog feet following the dotting
Of the stars:
Succumb
Without question
Serve to be served.

No one here but me and the mountains
The paths full of bone and meat
Moving persons
Circling the aftermath
Of bombs
Which cleared
Their insides
Out—

Just the shape of the mountain
Is enough love
Speaking it writes
A resurrection of the tribes
Hidden in disguise—
If the wind blows right
And you are looking.

Windows of the Panorama

Your eyes are in my head
Like a mountain morning,
Rising heat and light—
Every sixth wave is you
Your fingers on the lips
Of the poem—
As the afternoon you came
Full
A concerto of dreams
The senses drumming a
New guitar
Your knees parallel to
Your eyes
The fecundity of your hair
In a dance
A passage leading to the
Higher elevations of the
Panorama
Which through dresses of shades
Arrived at its darkest night
Gown
Your tongue of sweet pineapple
With a flirt of coco—
It was then that through a
Larger melody of ingredients
Our eyes ran into the nature
Of themselves
And locked like two owls—
Blood bones and soul
In the sight—

The vision a dictionary of
Boleros
I heard every limerick of
Invention—
As we sat under the umbrellas
Of the trees
The sea waving not too far
The moon above
A rich port
Of true revelation peeling
Trees in amorous growth
On the horizon
Flamenco.

Cohoba

The sky folds and enters your tongue,
The clouds become your teeth,
Your speech is rain
Going up to the moon
Her dark eyes come back with you,
You both see another face
The moon becomes embarrassed
Brings its people of shadows
Closer to the solar plexus
Together with the golden
Disk
Running off toward a cave,
In the darkest Eyelands
Now closed
The river becomes a light
That just stares at you
With its sound.

The Hammock

The Tainos of the Antilles
Invented the greatest apparatus
To make love in:
The hammock.
While all the other
Culture centers were
Producing philosophers,
Telescopes,
Pyramids

And modern man has
Gone on to invent:
Radios, televisions,
Nuclear bombs,
Agent orange,
Yellow dye #3,
The hamburger and pizza.

Taino engineering
Dedicated itself to the basics,
The height of its ingenuity said:
Happens what happens
On the hammock
You can go right down
To the bone.

Yjuanas

There's not an iguana that isn't drawn up
First on ocean abalone shell tinges of color,
Some with splashes of azules and pinks,
Around their waist a Matisse of blue,
Achiote feet crawling out of topaz sand dunes,
Umbrellas of crimson amapolas,
Despite the Yankees a grace from Areyto singing
Right through all malfunction.
A motion takes transport in guiro circles
If life has left society
The singers claim there are ears
Alive in river rocks by night and day
From which Yjuanas gowns
Dive toward baptism
Legs scrambling through waterfalls.
What the eyes of the bamboo flute sees,
A reptile sees
Yjuanas picture
A place that can never be told in words.

Atmospheric Phenomenon:
The Art of Hurricanes

Out of Africa arises a silence
To dance with the sky—
Spinning it makes its music in the air
Follows the route of the drum,
Comes toward the Atlantic—
To drink rum in the tropic islets
To use the bamboo as flute.

Big horizon of space upset,
Traveling through moisture and heat,
It has been known to throw steps
Of 200 miles per hour—
And yet a man of the mountains
Observed a miniature orchid
Purple and yellow
Hold on with such a pride
That it withstood the hurricane—
To hang with the Christmas flora,
Months later in our hot winter.

Each hurricane has its name
Its own character—
Hugo was strong and clumsy,
His strokes were like Van Gogh—
Bold and thick.
Pellets that were punches against the doors.
He came in vortex spirals.
Painting the sky of "Starry Night"
Above us.

He was poignant like tropical fruit.
Devouring mangos and guavas at will.
Breadfruit which flavors the tongues of Malaysia,
Enriching the waists of the hula dancers
In the South Pacific whose belly buttons
Hear better than ears.

Breadfruit which fries or boils
Was rolling through the streets
Of small towns surrounded by mountains—
As if Hugo did the favor
Of going shopping for us
With free delivery.

The Lesser and Greater Antilles like
Keys on a saxophone
An acoustic shoot
Each playing their note.
Did he blow?
A high sea note
Crescendo-waves
Coastal blues.
An air of leaves,
A percussion of branches
In the melody
The sound of green.

As if an asteroid fell
From the heavens—
Making all the religious
Churchgoers
Hallelujah onto their knees

To pray in total fright
In the face of death,
As if all that church attendance
Was not enough
To give them the blessings
When finally God sent
An ambassador in the form of a cyclone.

Makes one see that
People act contrary
To the laws of science.

Iris was a bitch—
She flirted from 14° north latitude
To 19° north—zigzagging
Lateral west
All that stripteasing
And she didn't come.
She went north,
Beautiful Iris
With her almond eye—
Full of lusty gusts.

Marilyn had curves—
A buttocky volition,
An axial memory that went down
To her tail.
At first she was a mere
Gyrating carousel on
The horizon—
On the satellite picture
She looked like a splattered

Sunny-side-up egg.
Her eye small
Like a black frijol
A beany socket,
Searching for the Virgin Islands.

Maelstrom of the sky—
A piranha of Carib moisture,
Calypso in the middle eye—
A vision which is also breath.

A hurricane is the heartburn of the sky—
A schizoid space,
A rotating mill of nervous air.
What made it so worried?
How did it become so angry?
The atmosphere sneezes.
God bless you.

A necklace of esmeraldas,
The stairway of islands
We are sitting roosters
Waiting to be caressed
Our turquoise gown
Ripples in the wind.

Why was it that that Friday eve
When the hurricane was coming in
The beauty parlors were full?
Get dressed, María
Permanent your hair—
Luscious Caribee—

Extra starch
In case I hang my head out
To the breeze tonight.
Sand, palm, white rum
And perfume. A band
Of clouds for white shoes.

The islands look like spinach
That fell into a blender.
Whirlpool dancer
Licking the rim of the sun
Achieving the enlightenment
That comes through motion and moisture.

After Marilyn Saint Thomas
Was like a Jackson Pollock painting—
Telephone lines like a plate of spaghetti.
A canvas of pickup sticks
Covered with random-chance zinc roofsheets
Automatic rhythm art of happens improve—
A colorful square of inspiration.

Saint Croix was in the joy of Kandinsky's
Brush,
Lateral strokes pushing the sky
To collapse into molasses.

In the howling screech a thought:
Have the stars been blown away?

Caribbean islands
Sprinkled in the form

Of a crescent moon
Falling into Venezuela,
The land of Simón Bolívar,
The Orinoco
Currency of our blood.

A hurricane clears the earth's
Nasal passages
A hurricane would do Los Angeles some good—
The winds of Luis
Could have been packaged
In banana leaves,
Its eyeball of great
Cinematropic suggestion
Placed right outside Beverly Hills,
Driving through the freeways
Breaking the speed limit,
A vacuum of 100-mile radius
Dispelling contamination—
The picture in motion.

Tainos knew that palm Bohíos
Were portable homes—
When the tempest came
To remove them—
In two days they had them
Back up.

As the wind roars
Like a million ghosts—
Hurakán lingua accents each letter.
Going through in total disrespect

Of industry and technology
And conventional itinerary,
Things disappear.

Hurricanes go west
Then north to be cool.
A spirit which knocked
Down Antillean coconuts
Could still be breeze
Cooling tea in Scotland.
My dear Lord—
What passes through
A fruit of passion—
To sniff among the English.

The horizon was a bowl
For Marilyn to make her stew—
Stir in the escabeche
The ocean soup.
Ancient appearance
Would have been
Below in caves.
Subterranean Church
Next to the hidden river
Flowing in peace—
Allowing the passage
Of Hurakán—
Bowing in respect.

Time Zones

Time is crying upon the backs of lizards,
Through the white stone of the medieval city
They dash.
The houses that are walking up the stairs,
Flowers out of ruins,
Further into the fortress,
The sounds of a language registers
In our dreams.

Words which are my hat in the city,
Coming through the bamboo
The shadows of lost meaning—
Tilted light making slivers
Through the forest of the mambo
Behind the eyes.

Time will shine your head into skull
The circle song will come again and again,
If we forget how to lay out a village,
Just open a guayaba in half,
These seeds are perfect,
And can guide you back,
Your hands the electric of the ghosts,

In the Persia of shining alfombras,
A belly button silks upon a horse,
Enters a tent of rhythms,
Makes the trees dance into shape,
Rubén Darío saw them in the river,
Bathing in the echoes of the castles,

His Indio head,
Clean enough to measure
The tempo of a camel,
The first string that vibrated
The Rock of Gibraltar,
To sway Greco-Roman lips,
Arising fire of Gypsy song,
Was making Castile dress and undress,
With the sounds that were hitting the moon
And falling down unto earth as colors.

Of boats that were my shoes.
Atlantic cha-cha-chá.
Splicing through 101st Street brick.
Which covered dancing verdure green
Rectangular mangos,
Cylindric bananas
Sounds in the sky blue tropic: mind.

Trees are making maracas
That will soon make you dance,

Water is their god of cadence,
As I sea walk through coconut heights,
Legs of tamarind,
Purple orchids arranged like syllables,
Insects of the morning dew sting verses on café.
In embroidery of Italians,
Garcilaso came to José Martí,
Who ducked Spanish spies
In Manhattan
And hugged Walt Whitman's beard in Philadelphia

As the Cuban Habaneras' Shango
Made it south to tango.

Boats are ages sailing on the water,
Parrots are flying out of castanets,
Flamenco peeling pineapples
That go up the river,
The water that became El Quijote's language,
As a cane field disappears into a bottle,
To awake in a little town
With molasses orbiting the cathedral,
A wooden saint slicing through the
Mountain full of potassium radiation,
Slanted plátanos pointing into medieval
Liturgy,
Bongo and ocean waves carving
Phantasmal antiquity
Through the fabulous language
That has taken the shape of
An Andalusian rhyming door,
One after the other.
Perfume pagano
Sailing out of the archways,
As Ricardo Ray turns into a centipede,
Marching across a Brooklyn piano,
For dancers to Sanskrit their
Gypsy feet,
Upon Albaicin ceramic tile.
Caribbean sun melts the caramel,
Making our first national flag:
White skirts waving in the air.

Machetes taking off like helicopters
Chopping off branches for timbale sticks,
The hands of the sun hitting the
Moon like a drum—
Making the atmosphere of moisture
Heat up,
For the chorus of the song
To come back down polinizando
The carnival flower,
A serenade walkilipiando.

Sliding upon seashells,
That disappear into the foam of time,
One age living next to another,
We are both living things at once,
We are the cadaver that is
About to be born.

If You See Me in L.A. It's
Because I'm Looking for the Airport

to John Daley and Lewis MacAdams

Even without Hollywood
It would still be an invention,
An imperialist drama from the
Spaniards to the Gringos,
Some automobile Hopalong Cassidy,
Arty hillbillies doing 90
On the San Bernardino
It's like a baker drops you
In the middle of the dough
Of the rising angel cake.

What is it, just a script in motion.
A performance,
Cameras rolling without text
So far through Sunset Boulevard to get
To an idea—
A Russian corner
A certain Gorky that salvaged beer.

What city,
A wiring of freeways, suburbos,
Only when you turn the TV on
The news convinces you that
There might be an attachment.

Billboards
So that perhaps if you're doing
Eighty you could look at them.

The relationship of people to
Their TV is a perversion
In the pocket of some
Beverly Hills cat psychiatrist—
Lap cats forced to sit with
Owners dizzied from remote control.

Don't get me wrong:
There are great literary geniuses
Practicing dialogue for be-cool movies
Try reading that enviro/mental snarl
From a Caribbean balcony
Things people say down the street
In spontaneous coconut drops
Finds parking in the lot
Next to proverbs
And rhythms.
More than cheeseburgers
Gay or those that drive straight
Off Maliboo
Speed I can't get to,
I am deprived by distance,
A barbarism that Jajuyas
So far from Rome—
An immigrant eternity
Should that make it unique,
Is that a third of the planet
Outside the doors of San Juan

L.A. is constant May Day
Residential barns
Off of constantly circulating

Traffic—
Wide enough so that you are
Not crowded by the slave
Quarters of looney tunes,
Utility living in mind,
Just keep the body running
Like a '57 Chevy.

Every ten years everything
Starts all over again.
If it were not for the oldies
What landmarks would there be?
The place would only have a future,
Nothing happening yet—
It's coming.
Can I park your car?
Can I take your order?

Car flirting
Car sex
Ah, if I get that chrome
What gets out of them
Diminishes.

I have fond memories of L.A.
Getting-lost stories on a pile,
The kind of off-the-track
Where you run out of gas
And can't find a gas station.

What would the Mexicans want
L.A. back for?

They got Mexico City
And can give lessons
On how to perfect
The pollution.

So if you have survived
The image of your own image—
Perhaps you see something
Walking outside your windshield,
A mural of Huichol geometros
Giant Mayas up on project walls,
A Guatemalan woman carrying
A bag balanced on her head down
Pico Street climbing some stairs
To a blue-coated apartment
Where Mayan corn
Hangs like framed saints.

A chanting that is old
In doo-wop radio,
The palms of the hands
Playing eternity upon
Tortilla flats,
A bridge over a river
That refuses to die
Linking what is not lost,
With what will not survive.

Now I see it in the rear
View mirror
La Virgen de Guadalupe

I gave my flowers to
Upon a wall
Like a gate into the East Side
A little brown boy and girl
Holding hands
Clutching tamales
As they walk toward Brooklyn
Of the urban Michoacán,
Now the ultra-new buildings
are smaller
Than the shine of the
New World eyes
Beholding the distance
Of the smog.

LETTERS FROM THE ISLAND

To my daughter Kairi and children everywhere

To Kairi

Are you speaking Spanish?
So that next time you come
You can talk with your
Girlfriends
Remember the game where
You clap your hands and sing—
As if the words were in the palms.
The language where you are is English
But in your house they sometimes
Speak Spanish—
It sounds like something warm and round
It sounds like love—
Spanish like feathers in air
Romantic.

I think of the two languages
I write in both
In one I find something
That I can't find in the other
I make a little bridge
I can walk across the bridge
All day long.

To me Spanish seems round
and vegetable—
English is vertical and goes
Straight up into the air
Like cylindrical pipes—
In English it is like being inside
walls—

Spanish is outdoors and circles.
When I go outside I see words
Walking around the streets—
Spanish words have soft tips
Syllables that melt into each other
They dress in fresh cotton
Spanish is full of agricultural glances
Harvest rhythms of Jíbaro dances
To make words dance valse
Under orange trees.
Look at a map of Latin America
In Cuba, Puerto Rico, and Santo Domingo
People speak Spanish.
Look now to where Mexico begins
Keep going down all of Central America
And on to South America—
All those countries sing in Spanish.

So you should practice your Spanish
Think of all the countries you can
Speak it in.
If one language is good
Two is more flavors
Don't forget your Spanish—
Through the cold nights of the north,
Next time you are down here
I'll take you by the hand
And in Spanish you can
Tell me the names of things
As if for the very first time.

II

Folk songs and what they say
are the true old feelings
Of a people
Of the land where one's eyes
First saw the light—
As if the trees and flowers
Were growing inside of you
Rocks and flowing rivers
Mountains and fruits
Birds and zillions of insects.

Even the movement of hands tells stories
From mouth to ears
In the air a song can live
For generations—
You can sing what your grandmother sang
As she walked amapola-lined paths
A song is sound in wind
That's its true house—
A bird in your chest
Your heart is a hammock
Waving Amor
Attached to palms that drum.

Kairi, we will go to Ponce
The pearl of the south
Home of the musical rhythm
Plena because we are African
Beats walking in the future
Of the past modern city towns
Doing in chorus
A verbal radio lip telegraph

In Ponce a neighborhood
They say that San Anton
That is where the plena was born
Whatever happens could be
Put into a song
Little episodes of life
Remembered and told
Singing musicians walking the streets
Daily newspapers printed in ears
The rhythm catches fire
As feet go after goats
Stretched upon hand drums
Going to the fiesta—
Following the songs that are
The true old feelings of a people
As if right then and there
You were being made—
Song is something that always is
And always will be
Listen:
The voice is yourself.

Water from a Fountain of Youth

Ah, to be fifteen and Latin from Manhattan walking around the Avenue D housing projects with a portable transistor radio listening to the Symphony Sid show, with a copy of William Carlos Williams's *Selected Poems* stuffed into your back pocket. Turning a street to the beat of Charlie Palmieri and the Charanga Duboney, heading toward Tompkins Square Park, where a group of conga-bongo-timbale drummers were holding summer sessions centering the Cuban son, in northern annex, which had been well appropriated from way back before when Machito's Afro-Cubans had the congregation at La Conga Club shining the floor, transporting an antique sacred pounding into the bustle of Manhattan. Cuban poet José Martí angled poems in the West Side cold, which now Juan Tanameras everywhere in the popular song or when El Teatro Puerto Rico up in the Bronx was bringing in popular entertainment from all over the Americas, like the time they brought the Mexican movie star and singer Antonio Aquilar complete with his horse. They had the horse tied up on a side street around 139th Street feeding it hay—some noise got the horse upset and it took off running up Brook Avenue, and the whole crew had to go after it. Bronx streetcorner machos were climbing up fire escapes. All these things I heard when I was young and hungry to eat the city as a salad of buildings and windows, brick bread. To be young and off of 10th Street hearing that son that Nicolas Guillen made a line through, in my Conversational sneakers of poetry, floating on out through *Kora in Hell* of magnified building lights. The hands of the drummers chopping like speech. Listening to the flowing talk, poetry the river in the language. Fragments of English, chips of Spanish. The sound of the language a cubist painting. The

Latin-Arabic tongue splish-splashing and sliding through the tongue the Pilgrims came here talking, whereas 100 years before the Mayflower Puritans, San Juan was a city jumping with the first mestizos opening new Spanish vocabulary mixed with Arawak fruit pulp. Mayagüez was far enough from San Juan to cultivate a disregard for authority that persists in the city known as Princes of the Turks—western ledge of the island where a famous North American poet's mother was born, Elena Hobeb. Williams listening to his mother describes it in his book *Yes, Mrs. Williams:* "Words and sayings intermixed fascinated me the more. I began to copy down her phrases. I collected all kinds of notes." Williams stayed Americano, his friend Eliot swam to Europe, Pound went to Italy. Was it that turn-of-the-century Puertorriqueña Elena that influenced his native speech poetics? Her form of memory in the Spanish voice, her English scramble. Upper-class Mayagüez woman who spoke in tongues and made him beans. Dr. Williams drove and wrote as he flashed through the streets toward a patient. El Doctor wrote between the labor pains of mothers. As a pediatrician he brought some 3,000 babies into the world. Carlos a street-walking poet of my early pérdidas.

To confront the Caribbean Spanish of Nicolas Guillen—a poet who heard the voices in the air of Camagüey, Cuba, bemba on paper—was to wish that there were more curves in the Teutonic base of English. Maybe the thing to do is to squash it a little, pull it by the hair of the syllables, put the words into a pilón y maseta chop, giving the Germanic a stretch into a horizontal line, putting curry curves like they did in India into that vertical pensive sensation of the English. In that manner, words were bouncing off the bricks, broken syllables could become wholes, the poems could take dance steps toward song, a cadence flowering through the urban structures, taking concepts and imagination into the talking tongue, continuing the Caribbean posture of a multiplicity of things happening at the same time. Guitars melting into chekeres. Everybody's simultaneous yakkity-yak. What you hear is like a wall coming down to your face. A mandala of mouths eating everything. Imagine the paintings of the faces emitting from that racial melange, facial feature anarchy, new lips for a new world, gene painting. Wilfredo Lam landscape bush in orbit around Hieronymus Bosch. Spanish/English: two systems to make streets of sounds, with buildings full of staircases, producing knots, words well combined are hall/ucinogens creating holograms on city walls.

What's more is that my early poetic intentions were influenced by the Puerto Rican tradition of declaiming from memory. That was how I first heard poems proclaimed. Those poems that came out of the Spanish language all rhymed, many were being brewed by then in Latin American countries. So there I was in New York in the mid-sixties trying to write in these meters of the Castilian copla, the Italian ottavilla, which many moons back had invaded Spain. Trying to find rhymes in English, it's like trying to find banana leaves for pasteles in Ann Arbor, Michigan. Difficult plainthing (or plaintano) it could just be twistly congested, the heat of the poem could go into shock through the chill of the long search for a correspondent sound. Not to offend Keats, who beats on time, jumps and bumps into rhyme time so well and tell, but he was on home turf from mother's milk. Spanish coplas found it difficult to settle into the English duplex, something had to be done to find the sound of my force feet theme.

It was Lorca's *Poeta en Nueva York* that helped to water the seed of verse libre, 'cause he kept clave and took solos too. He was like I was: traditional and experimental at the same time, rooted in folk patterns, song, dance, music, giving the words wings. I was embracing the poets who had song and music orientation and taking that spacing into literature. Poets of folkloric research like Antonio Machado, poets who were between song and paper. Latin American composers of boleros, Agustín Lara flipping over the metaphors of Rubén Darío in such a beautiful plagiarism. The other approach is to see poetry as merely literate, conceptual and discursive, all things that Caribbean popular culture is not. This is not a favoring of one approach over the other but a search for the encounter point. Reading how the earth appears in the poems of Miguel Hernández, the Spanish poet Franco allowed to die in a jail. Blood in the poetry of Lorca. My early readings of those poets helped my voice walk the sing-song expression coming down from the mountains into the streets. Many offsprings of classical cultures came to the Caribbean: the Spanish, and by extension the Greco-Roman world; the Yoruba, Bantu, and other cultures from Africa; the Arawak-Taino base, and by extension the whole world of indigenous America. So Caribbean cultivation truly is a work of balancing of simultaneity. In the poetry of Derek Walcott there is a comfortable link between the calypso and Greek myths. The agua-zuli horizon of his mind piercing a line between disparate yet complementary classical outlooks. (God is talking to the individual directly.) Caribbean like that is. That's what I look for in a finely wrought poem, a discussion between meditation and action. The street and the library. Lorca walking with the Gypsy down Broadway. The al-Andaluz camel prancing through Castile.

Poetry is the sound of air in your head. To make it into language is a translation; that's still within the same language. To translate it to the page or the voice is another translation. To use a different language, or two languages in stereo, is a translation of a translation of a translation. To translate is to migrate, to read. But much more wonderful than hearing it is migrating back to where it was related. That's where I am now, mixing it. And in the Caribbean, where things are already mixed, literature is walking, poetry dancing. All I need is a canoe to start following the embroidery of the rhythms of the peoples of the river. Poetry is a river in the language. Paddle and you will get there.

Writing Migrations

Language could have originally been a silent awareness—an interior communication with a different matrix dimension, a compass to pinpoint our cosmological position. Slowly we came into the sounds of flowers. Languages all related in the bone opened up like a fan across territorial landscapes. Exile and bilingualism have merged once again the tones of our flesh, creating tension and drama at the confluence of the meltdown. This is the undertow of history. The population in transit creates and evolves cuisine, music, new vocabulary, mixing the aesthetics of a homeland with the newly acquired visual and audio espectáculos. The United States is the hottest spot of ethnic and linguistic debate today. This churning we are experiencing is the true center of human society. What is stagnant, what is dormitory, what is truly in opposition to oxygen is monoculture, monolanguage, monorhythm. It is a point of nonexistence, diminishment. We are living nothing but the true cycle of history. Didn't the Greeks Alexandria into Egypt? Writing is motion from the local toward all unseen correspondences.

Everything we see has memory. No two people are seeing the same thing—all mangos have a variation to their taste. Translation is only transportation of meaning; the fire of music stays within each native tongue. You wouldn't know when to laugh out of insinuation. Language is timing, a cadence. Everyone is not in the same present; we are inside mandalas with points of different time zones circling each other. Recognizing words does not mean that we are feeling them. Words have to be felt to draw the maximum out of them— there are always meanings beyond anything we can find in the dictionary. It could be that you are the only one who perceives a lion in the room; everyone else is reposed in cake.

Language comes from the feet to the mouth. It is felt in one's shoes as well as in one's belly—it comes from inside and outside, an atmospheric condition. It is inside of trees and in the glass windows of buildings, in the eyes and in the waves. It is pantomime and speculation, walk and dance, the way an old man holds a cane, the way a young woman folds and slightly lifts her dress. Semantics is a rumba of birds in flight over Utuado or any distant town in this global wrapping. Each language sound spectrum is a different dream that makes a person walk up to oneself. Talk of air, bone, flesh in the choreography of understanding. Grasp through sound and color, and fragrance, touch direct taste of a state, the pinpoint of sabor by the very flute of the fleshy muscular organ of taste and voice: LENGUA/TONGUE. The same for it to jump out into the air as to submerge into the darkness of one's base.

To translate is to find an equivalent difference. There is no actual translation but an approximate presentation of the contents unfolding. Having grown up bilingually, I now have an accent in both Spanish and English.

Migration and bilingualism, the companions of my poetry, are also present in the poets I teach. They all share this intense duality. Thinking about it further, I wonder what poetry or world literature would not be in this wonderful dilemma. Looking at buildings I see mountains: in Manhattan, the square tits of Cayey. The shift to the north always seems to imply the transformation of globes into rectangles.

Bilingualism could come about as a result of political upheaval, imperialism, migration, exile—all are related. It could be imposed or adopted. Most classrooms in U.S. cities are now showing this human hodgepodge, each face a beat in world music. Things are coming together to create tensions, and combinations that will result in new forms to respond to the variety produced by the chessboard of history.

Seeing two languages collide, melt, struggle, fight, sabotage each other is one of the greatest shows on earth—the sensations that feed and stimulate writing come right along with linguistic warfare. Literature becomes history, physical and psychological forces alive in words. Stories and poems are chronicles of migration, syllables of adjustment. Our original language changes but it does not disappear. The present physical location is always mixed with what has disappeared—this is the state of poetry itself, the science of metaphor, the constant sway of what is with what isn't. This idea of things being out of place is, for me, a very interesting sharp jolt. The contrast of tropicality and cold northern urbanity makes for what some might describe as surrealism, but I am not going out of my way to distort or make a reality that is not an everyday occurrence. It is a movement through the physical and the psychological, an iceberg in the north whose hidden region is a rain forest, parrots swinging from palm to page. Through memorial glances I could see avocados falling into the snow.

Bilingualism and geodisplacement are what makes poetry not just something we find in books, but the very path that each student uses to get to the classroom. It jumps out in the street, in the jungle encountered walking down Fifth Avenue. What else could make the imagination take such a leap?

Is this not the twentieth century, where one could be in an igloo in Alaska watching on a portable t.v. a movie showing scenes of Manhattan streets? These kinds of contradictions are deeply poetic.

Observers can articulate the oddity of the movement, the opposition and encounter of recipes, methods, and ways of doing things. The most obvious contrast is the rural and the urban—poetry can become a discussion about how towns and villages became cities—about how we crossed from the nineteenth into the twentieth century—about gadgets made by machines and objects made by hands. We must never forget that poetry is written in the head and then transported to the world by the hand. I always write with pen and paper first, feeling the waves of my thoughts, which immediately move the muscles of my arm and hand to write, a form of breathing and scribing at the same time. It is thus a craft that comes about one letter at a time. It combines the chronology of a private life with history, mixes the elements of the future into the present. It is different time zones orbiting simultaneously and in close proximity. Writing is the oil spill of memory. Imagination, the memory of the future.

In the writings of many Latinos in the United States there is a great grasp of this dislocation, geoconfusion, territorial crisscrossings—an inquiry into the nature of place. When speaking of Latino writing in English or Spanish, this point must be driven home. In the north we feel a consciousness cultivated in a different climate. Because of the close proximity of the two Americas, a good portion of the Latinos in the u.s. will always look like they just got off the boat. Even twenty years from now this will be the case. We are eternal aliens, we might as well be Omnis. Just recently I saw a Guatemalan woman walking down Sunset Boulevard in Los Angeles balancing a bag of groceries on her head as she stepped on the walk of stars. In his poem, "Frutas," Cuban American poet Ricardo Pau Llosa gives us this awareness of the seesaw experience:

> Growing up in Miami any tropical fruit I ate
> could only be a bad copy of the Real Fruit of Cuba.
> Exile meant having to consume false food,
> and knowing it in advance. With joy

my parents and grandmother would encounter
Florida-grown mameyes and maimitos at the market.
At home they would take them out of the American bag
and describe the taste that I and my sister
would, in a few seconds, be priviliged to experience for
the first time.

This charming discovering of fruits out of their climate brings into focus a lot of Chicano, Puerto Rican, and Latino poetry; suggests ways to approach a literature which has its five senses in constant flight from the immediate downtown.

Forget about history textbooks; poems are the best way to study and teach history. Poems are testaments of the actual experience of living through a personal and public event; they are the closest thing to the truth. Historical writing is what might have happened, what people have said over and over again, or what historians have written, being reflected upon by others ad infinitum. The voice of an epoch is in the words of its poets. Poetry is synonymous with exile in Latin America. Eccentrics who deviate from conventional behavior in rural campesino communities feel the pressure and are soon isolated. The Peruvian poet César Vallejo got the message quickly, and after being thrown in jail for some triviality, he headed for the metropolis. He didn't stop there; he went right through the border and headed to Europe. Vallejo's book *Trilce* represents the struggle of a mestizo experience in ardent linguistic awareness; that is, there seems to be a battle in the ordering of the perceptions in the Spanish language, a constant ricocheting with the indigenous corridors of his being, which makes for the beauty and the difficulty of his poems. I never teach him in the classroom, but I do point him out when speaking of Latin American poets and their condition of exile from their homelands. In Paris he saw the Andes towering beyond the Eiffel Tower.

If we read and teach Latin American poetry, we should do it with a keen sense of history. In most cities there are great libraries that have stored away archives of Latin American periodicals and magazines. It would be most effective if the class, while reading the poems of José Martí or Rubén Darío, could peruse xerox printouts of newspapers and magazines published around the time of the production or publication of the poems, in the native countries or regions where the poets traveled. The Latin American poets I cite have all been translated into English in various editions. The Nicaraguan poet Rubén Darío is a good example of a poet in motion. In his poetry there are great geographic sweeps. Born in Metapa (now Ciudad Darío) surrounded by cacao and palm trees, his poetry is full of Greek statues, Mount Parnassus, French streets, and words. He left, imaginatively and physically, the tropics of his birth to write a structured and poignant poetry that nonetheless is both Nicoya and international in scope. A discussion and an understanding of this Latin American spiritual aesthetic should be inspired in the students of literature. This wandering from country to country was the destiny of many Latino poets, as it was for the indigenous tribes of the Americas. Indigenous tribes having left the Orinoco basin, canoeing and splashing in piraguas down rivers and across oceans, they traversed the island of Borinquen, appearing on a Mayagüez beach two months later. This experience persists with contemporary Latinos.

This motion, this tremendous coming and going, this here and there, is captured by Latino poetry, art, and music. It is really serious—ask anybody. Students can write poetry from the point of view of a suitcase. Rubén Darío's poetry could be read as a globe. If articles from *La Nación,* a famous Argentinian periodical, could be made available to the class, history and literature would unite. Expression is the encounter of the personal with the temperment of the epoch. It was while reading an article by José Martí published in Argentina that Darío first became aware of the poetry of Walt Whitman. Without reading a single line of Whitman's poetry, he wrote his famous "Ode to Walt Whitman." It is amazing what a group of words can suggest. It could have been the age of the Big Stick policy in Washington but poets wanted to communicate across borders and languages. What if we could bring this alive to a class of recent arrivals from Cambodia, Santo Domingo, El Salvador, Chile, etc? They can see that the journey of their families is analogous to the movements of poets and their poems. Migration is usually necessary to escape drought, poverty, or bombs, but a popular refrain states: "Al mal tiempo buena cara." In San Francisco I visited many schools full of students who have come from many different and troubled lands. Inside each memory there is a tale of an exodus. Two exposures always exist within the space of a single photo. A duality opens up in front of you—part urban, part rural—part brick, part mango. In that constantly swinging pendulum, in that encounter between oddities, in that yin and yang have always rested the sources that bring out and sharpen talent. Visitations come to the language we speak and write: volcanos, anacondas, alpacas, mameyes, in the crepuscular air, waves of New England frost, the singing of the coquís. The sharp differences and distances between things becomes their beauty at the instant of their merger. Guarani canoes appear in the lake at Central Park.

The Cuban critic Antonio Benetez-Rojo, in his book *The Repeating Island,* describes the Caribbean as organized chaos, a place where all the societies, cultures, and races have come to rotate around each other, mixing and melting, no one staying in their original racial or aesthetic position. Which is not to say that the culture does not contain pockets where one form is stronger or purer than the other. That too. Where things meet, though, it is unpredictable and varied and moves with a certain strut. That is what we can say of the poetry. Lots of things will come to mind—pictures which want to be painted as words, horrible thoughts as in nightmares, unspeakable inclinations we never share with anyone. They are beats which have to be organized by the drummer. At the same time we respect that percentage of any given experience that can never be tamed. There is beauty in that raw rain forest. It is not the fault of a hurricane that they have decided to construct large structures with glass windows in the Caribbean. That fury in the wind is the god Hurakán. The events that manifest themselves in nature also declare themselves in us: revolution, migration, exile. Benetez-Rojo describes chaos in conjunction with the scientists of this new theory: ". . . that is, Chaos to mean that within the (dis)order that swarms around what we already know of as Nature, it is possible to observe dynamic states or regularities that repeat themselves globally." Stravinsky tried to write down the beats of a rumba session in Havana but he couldn't hang, yet there is great pattern and form in the rumba, there is a centering that rotates. To me, that is writing also, so many angles coming to meet in this public celebration, because writing to me is not an alone-lonely-private affair. How could it be?—we are using the language of humanity. All the words except the ones we invent ourselves are in the dictionary. The center in the Caribbean is waves and mountain curves going every which way. It has got to be the greatest show on earth. One could truly say everything is everything. The surprises never stop, they come one right after the other.

From the rhythms of these floating islands have come great poets to love them even if they had to leave them. I have taught the poetry of José Martí (1853-1895) at the university level, and each leafing through his poems or poking through his adventurous life was like the unfolding of a movie. Because of Martí's ardent conviction that Cuba should be free of Spanish colonial rule, he was imprisoned and soon after sent into exile by the authorities. Like other Latin American poets, many of his most Cuban poems were written on the road. Often the sense of place of those displaced is greater than those in place. Exile is the aerial view. The geographic emotion, faces, fruits, rivers, and balconies come to our memorial windows, poems full of volcanos and earthquakes, guava trees uprooted and flying through the air of the hurricane's concert. In Martí one could see with great clarity how history deposits itself inside a poet. From the very beginning of his writing life, when he published the short book *Ismaelillo* (1882), a series of poems that he wrote in Caracas for his son back in Cuba, Martí bagan to swallow the whole panorama of the Americas. He came through the Spanish language like an ice breaker. In his language a real individual is present, his metaphors are not worn clichés, his language is not flowery or customary. He found a way to link his private passion to his social vision. His poems have short breaths, immediate thoughts. He was well read in both Spanish and English. He knew Spain from its air to his foot. He knew what was right and what needed to be overhauled in his heritage. His essay "Nuestra America" is a good companion piece to his poems. Those who can read his Spanish will note that there is a tremendous amount of poetic somersaulting in his prose. The discussion concerning what a person is in relationship to a society will take center stage.

Reading about Martí's life, I could now close my eyes and see him walking through the streets of the Lower West Side during the latter half of the nineteenth century. Occasionally he and other members of the Cuban Revolutionary Party had to dodge the spies the Spanish government would send. It was on a cold winter street in New York where Martí first met the poet Rúben Darío. Martí embraced the younger man and called him *Hijo,* taking Darío along with him to a meeting of Cuban and Puerto Rican revolutionaries clamoring for the end of Spanish colonialism.

Latin American literary history unfolded way beyond its borders—in the northern extremity of a city with a British name. José Martí wrote many of his great poems in the Catskill Mountains of New York—"I am a sincere man from where the plam trees grow"—as he looked out onto a rural wintry landscape.

Federico García Lorca has always been of interest because of his connections with Gypsy and Arabian culture, because he was well rooted in folklore and song. He cultivated the measure of traditional Spanish poetry and the passion of the Gypsy flamenco. His poems create sensations much greater than the meanings they register as if he were pushing colors through the air. His *Romance Gitano* is a great display of imagination within structure. In the book *Poeta en Nueva York,* Lorca experiments and improvises as he lets the new industrial urbanity take him places. There is such a thin line between Lorca's words and song that his poetry has been effortlessly transferred into music. Poets who are inspired by popular music and song are always fresh water for poetic seeds. We can see in Langston Hughes's poetry a relationship to the blues, in the poetry of the Cuban Nicolas Guillen a connection to Son, and Bob Kaufman's poetry to jazz. The breath of Luis Pales Matos's lines skip around in pursuit of the beat of the barrel drums of the Puerto Rican bomba. Play music so that you can hear the instruments suggesting line breaks. Reading these poets, you will realize that poetry is not produced in great solitude, it is not the sullen activity that is seems to those that are outside of the task. It is another of the popular forms integrated to dance, song, gossip (bochinche), and carnival. To read Lorca's *Poeta en Nueva York* is to experience the reactions of a pastoral being to the rush and sounds of industrial urban civilization. His visit to New York produced a creative tension similar to that felt by contemporary u.s. Latino poets in their own geographic and cultural displacement. Lorca is a point of confluence—there are so many differences that collide within him and that he sings and unifies, even while enjoying the contradictions. An unconscious and uneducated wholeness, an immediate reaction to earth and air, the peasant peoples of the world all share these attitudes. Poets and cultures are in exile. Hindu rhythms are out of place and intact in the Andalusian flamenco.

Exile and bilingualism are strong episodes in the life of writers. Examples abound throughout the history of literature. Joseph Conrad was born Polish but wrote in English after much seafaring, during which he picked up tidbits of port-of-call vocabulary and studied English. Writers have been linguistic immigrants well before other segments of society. Vladimir Nabokov wrote and published in Russian before he came to the states in 1940. Samuel Beckett was born Irish and wrote mostly in French. Cabrera Infante, the Cuban novelist who now lives in England, has done some writing in English, beginning with *Holy Smoke,* a book about tobacco lore and popular culture. Writing in a language other than one's first language can free one's thoughts and open up expressiveness. It moves one away from local customs, regionalisms, family phobias, the temptation

127

to use established refrains and personal clichés. Perceptions have no laws of grammar. Across the map of creation poets have served as translators. Robert Dole's recent suggestion that the United States pass an English-only law would put many U.S. poets out of business. No other literature had been so infused with foreign words. Ezra Pound's *Cantos* has most of the languages of the world represented in it, if not in practice, then in theory. Robert Hass's poetic task is to translate and reproduce in English the Japanese haiku. The novels of Elmore Leonard and Robert Stone are sprinkled with Spanish.

A distinction must be made between the bilingualism that is a writer's interest in other languages and the bilingualism that is imposed affecting an entire group of people, a whole culture. It would be best for a growing person to be fully competent and secure in one language before going out to embrace another. Too many word-sound possibilities could create delayed reactions in naming objects and responding to ideas. This process, if not checked or handled right, can create not bilinguals but nonlinguals. Those not competent and secure in either language. How can we make a literature with people who are not rounded out linguistically? I support bilingualism when two languages are able to strengthen each other and assist in expressive and imaginative flight but deplore bilingualism when it contributes to the degeneration of one of the languages, creating expressive confusion in a people. We don't need English-only or Spanish-only laws, we need English-plus and Spanish-plus. Experiments in Spanglish, the crisscrossing of the two languages, have to be taken one at a time. Some work, some don't—my preference nowadays is to see the two languages juxtaposed, each demonstrating their full beauty. Singular foreign words appearing in any poetic tradition are like beauty marks upon the body. In the courtyard gardens a rosa appears.

Exile, displacement, and bilingualism: the constant state of mankind, a source of great commotion and tragedy, and an experience of great revelation. All peoples, all times and all places are made up of this weaving. Caribbean and Latin American culture is in constant flux.

In the poetry of José Martí and Rubén Darío we can feel this great commotion. César Vallejo takes us to the core of mestizaje, the confrontation of two conceptions of reality coming out of one trumpet, disfiguring and melting the brass in the process. The conquest was like the Big Bang—the language shows the phosphorous explosion of thoughts, the jagged, the crooked, the beautiful. The rhythms are saying this as well— canto hondo coming out of rumba. Maracas, the instrument of the neolithic Caribbean, are played at Madison Square Garden. The islands are definitely repeating, appearing elsewhere, in different longitudes and latitudes. Poetry is most definitely emotion, and it is most definitely in motion.

Time Zones: The Junkyard

From a distance some fifteen antennas decorating the top of the Tropical Junk Shop are visible. One of them is actually connected to a shortwave radio that Monson claims to have found outside of a military installation, near the road leading to the guard house where they inspect what enters and leaves. Marifolio says that he likes seeing all those antennas jutting into the sky even if they don't work, 'cause they give the place the productive look of some kind of radio or television station. It makes him feel that he is into communication. Observed from certain angles, the antennas look like a scramble of Chinese characters. That is the observation that Marifolio lizards as we descend into town with a bird's-eye view of the shop and the yard. We had a long afternoon of shopping for balloons in San Juan.

"Look at all those antennas. It looks like Confucius is having a thought, Chinese characters standing up four-dimensionally."

"Or like one of those abstract paintings on exhibit at the university, if all that doodling could stand up vertically."

The inspiration of the Son montuno coming from the car radio was taking us into other realms, both electric and vegetative. Landing in the junkyard, drumming on the side of the Ford, we saw that all metals have sound for something good. If the Ford breaks down, we could just fashion cowbells out of its body, give them to that guy who percusses for the Sonora Ponceña. The clank of the cowbell resounds an octave above the cowhide stretched over the wooden frame of the conga drum.

Inside the junkyard Marifolio puts the balloons away for some future second wind. He sits down to fidget with the shortwave radio. He had added other receivers to it—progress, he thought, since that's the word of the land. It's a thirst that is forever changing the shape of things, the pull of repetitive profit. Elaboration of cord, migration of watt, the contradictions of electromagnetism, rejection and pull, escaping through the wire, the vibes of the disc jockey riding in on a horse of wax. The speakers that the shortwave radio are hooked up to— forget about them. Termination of cane. Atomic projection. The kind that the orchestras use in plazas to blast the people with rhythm. You can't come with no weak funnels, that plena has to be felt in the bone marrow. True it is that wherever a group gathers with a pandereta, a guiro and some mouths, people approach as if to a priestly command. That rich sound takes the poor out of Puerto. The speakers hooked up to the junkyard shortwave radio have an electrified legend. They go back to the days when the merengue was slower, before the metallic guiro came in with that screech and supersonic velocity, to when Mon Rivera gold-teethed to the mike with plenas that described everyday incidents in Mayagüez, the news of the lyrics unfolding before the eyes of the singer, the information molded between the spaces of trombones, drums, and maracas, an Antillean slap of palms in chorus, the borders holding the street corner together. So it was that one timba-slap made people dash out of doors, jump through windows, or from a distance shake to the unseen instruments, to rhythms that echoed off trees.

How did Mon Rivera's orchestra speakers come to reside within such a gathering of mutilated parts, the emergency room of fallen inventions? It has been traced back to a certain 1949 plena dance at El Club Los Leones that ended à la fists and slaps clean. Ironing out the wrinkles the next day, they say that too . . . but who knows who commenced the argument, something about a shoe, who to who, one to the other. They say that one of the dandies stepped on the other's white shoe that he had Griffined just for the occasion. Some had seen the dandy giving brush all afternoon to his shoes, listening to radio station Sal-Sol, liquifying himself into patterns of legwork, jumps of choreo riffs that a mirror reflected back, getting ready for the night. So that when that element came a-stepping on his shoe, he took it beyond the soles. How it must've rolled. The plena spinning, conversation and aroma. Silky yellow dresses buffing the lower pockets of guayaberas, folded handkerchiefs with blue lines held in moist hands pressed against the waists of the bailarinas, guiding in the shine, leading toward the left, moving toward the right, then in the middle, keeping it there, where, in the middle, there in the middle keeping it. Was it between numbers that the ple-ple added up? Girls fanning themselves so as not to catch fire. A plenatical spin comes to an end, two men walking with Indias in their hands. Due to the influence they miscalculate the motion of the foot on the step, and one of them throws too much, steps on the other's white shoe. They stand off. "Excuse me" is a useless phrase. Did the victim say: "For less they have died in Jagueyes." And the other, who was he the son of? Did he shoot back: "Tell me about it. Where I come from, they kill for a ball of white rice." It was the end of language. Their hands flew into each other. Screams start to erupt. Someone comes up to them to tell them: "Try talking about it. Avoid the manure." By then nouns could not get to the purity of the verbs. Cousins and uncles jumped like wood into the fire, creating a flame that made people stand on chairs, along with further murmur that rose. Plainly the bomb exploded. In the frenzy friends and family yelled for each other across the salon: "Hey, Flaco, get away from there." "I think it's time to go." "Hey, Malon, forget your beer from here, let's clear." All of that went like current through the crowd, so that what they say happened next is that the whole throng flew outside 'cause the melee had swollen, what with beer and testicles, a jump outside that the frogs couldn't imitate. The tumult jumped up on stage, and drums and maracas went flying, right down to the bass. Musicians dove in dreadful rhythms of dismay, leaving everything behind. Once outside they ate the dark space of the night as they dissolved into the oblivion of the boleros.

After the revolution had settled, it was discovered that instruments, speakers, and three cases of India beer were gone. Over the years details of the fray have fermented in the town into fracas folktales—the addition, the subtraction, the multiplication. They say that Mon Rivera's gold tooth was flashing like Morse code signals when he instructed his musicians to evacuate, that he lost no rhythm dashing across the floor and out, escorted into some Chevrolet. Tongues went listening about who had the trombone, lips went through filing cabinets, looking for who had the drums, the big congas that no one saw leave. And what of those giant stage speakers that were carried off? Could be that it was some wasn't that actually might have been. Whatever the case, the speakers changed hands many times over the years, an outlet for musical Caribbean stretch. Someone had to bring them finally to the junk shop for some wiring. Years of nonstop sound pouring through their veins.

When I asked Marifolio who it was, he said, "I don't know. I confuse the entity for all kinds of people. Was it Totin the Steamer, or one of the forty thieves of Ali Baba." Whatever the journey, there it was hooked into the current arriving from other worlds.

Indicating to Marifolio that it was time to study and not to work, as if studying was not a task, I flowed out, crossing the street, climbing the stairs, intent upon showering off the coastal sun, the ground war drive through the highway and streets of the capitol (after which who could go to work blowing up balloons and decorating a junk shop to make it look festive).

Revived and cleaned, I opened the pages of *La Colina de los Chopos*, Juan Ramón Jiménez's Madrid journal, the passages of which are alive and breathing on the Río Piedras campus. Waving in the paging afternoon the illuminings of that distant country, to which now a passing garza facilitates a Madrid panorama in which to land. According to Jiménez, all the poets of his generation were there champagning bubbles through the corridors of La Residencia de Estudiantes in Madrid, from which *La Colina* flows. That Vicente Machado'd Lorca in the blood-rich days of their verse. A space of encounters for poets who celestialed their words to resound above the branches of olive trees, to spill out in the grunts of sheep, a poetry that put grooves in the Rock of Gibraltar. Another leaf in Spanish opens up further visas of departure. Glancing across at the junk shop antennas imbibing the frequencies entering the shortwave receptors, it was clear that Marifolio was fingering the dial to reach some foreign song. Children's lullabies were coming from Moguer, the town in southern Spain next to the Río Tinto, where the fresh flow of the juice enters the deeper wine of the ocean. Platero through the window feeding an aspiration that all poets harbor to crawl out of the province, to dream out of the exhaust of habitat, even if it means licking a mountainside of rock to make it to the capital of their nation-hood. Jiménez's youth the native station of Moguer, before Madrid, the endurance of the province, before arriving in America, to San Juan, to discuss another garden visible from a classroom window.

Salvador Dalí the scroll juices painted the legs of Federico García Lorca's metaphors, a shampoo of medieval Catholic penitence breaking loose in the urbanity of expression, nice kids of the upper classes, the sons of lawyers masturbating into the Catholic alter chalice, boys in the drama of assisting the sacerdote. Within all that brushing and fountain pen caligrafía, Jiménez forged his language with an attention to jewels found in a concert of landscape. Abandoning a G string to the light of a J for the clarity of research, spoke the zound, manifested the zame. Across the street in the junkyard, on the waves rustling leaves rolling above antennas picking up whistles from the fruits of some Miami sixties rock 'n' roll station. It is clear that Marifolio is disintegrating on some space ship improvisation of a chair, across from where I travel and also see the immediate manifestation of what I am reading. Panorama. Landscape being the eternal in the poem, the naked dancers of fertility who shed their amapola skirts, the passage which will endure for as long as the mountains beckon the wind, the very caressing that will with time drown them once again. Lifting my eyes from the book to encounter all the light that sentiments upon a lizard's back as it fleets through a million years as if it were just an afternoon changing into the dark slip of eve. By perfect arrangement the radio, soft in the background, filters in the colors of a blind Rodrigo, Concierto Arunjuez, a slow bouquet of turning fragrances, the silence of nature itself deciding upon the tempos which will occupy it. The last note leaves the spectrum of music to become a halo. That's all I see as the locutor gives the time: 6:30. It is time to leave *La Colina de los Chopos* and book on back to work amongst the ruins. To blow color balloons.

Monson was in the shop now smoking away on some apparatus. As it was getting dark, the coquís were constructing their high rises, lining up in their nightly glee club. Each day at the touch of darkness the island's small toad population sets off its whistly chatter. How does it happen? Does one go off and signal the others awake? But could they hear? Are they just some mini-clocks always set to go off at nocturnal wind? Suppose the darkness didn't come out one weird evening, and they still take off and sing? For sure, we would know that they possess inner timing. All that frogology and insectology having intercourse while one reads or sleeps. What about during the daylight, when we don't hear or see them? Whatever it is that they insert must be in there, the song coming right out of the air, permeating all human motion, the sonance of their presence.

While Monson fingerprinted the details of an unidentifiable contraption, amphibian lust rose around the spoils of industry. He raised his head to ask: "Did you run into a gringa with a big sweet potato?"

"No, but the ugliest looking cop told us to leave town. I mean, he looked like an avocado that a cow tried to eat but spat back out. Anyway, we gotta blow up 3,000 balloons tonight so I hope you had your mondongo or mofongo or beanlongo." Marifolio versed with style from his searching dial.

Monson acted surprised, like he'd just been told to assist in the moving of a mountain.

"I see that shit in the direction of the inferno. 3,000 balloons —you'd have to hold that stuff up to a hurricane. 3,000 balloons—you gotta take it with ease. That sun was out kicking ass here. Maybe it rained where you were, but we got fried as usual. What d'you think this is, some kind of German machinist factory? What are you in a hurry for? Slow down. For what, to die? The world is big and plenty. Everybody's running with this progress charge. We could all start running into each other. Let's slow down and let those nuts who went off first fall down and collapse. Look, that's why this junk shop is full. This is nothing but a heap of progress. This is where all that stuff ends. What is it that that president of the United States says? The fuck ends here or the luck ends here? Whatever, you know what I mean. You can short-circuit trying to chase all this electricity."

"Monson, you talk and we blow. We gotta make some money this festival. For one, I'm planning a trip to New York, visit my family, see if I can find Inez too. And those books for school are costing some money, especially the ones published in Spain. You'd think we'd get a discount, given all the gold they took out of here."

"I'm going to blow. You just gotta take it easy. You get some place too fast, you think you're magic, or something that ain't. Let a son of a whore walk four miles to a place on foot; if he still has energy to be arrogant, call for the devil 'cause that might be his mother. I would spill out running, won't see me for a week. Look over at that bag; tell me there isn't a bottle of rum and kenepa juice in there, brewed up where the mountain enters heaven, made by Ferotin. 3,000 balloons—are you insane? Must be an off larger than a pipe with seven levers. You start blowing balloons now, I gotta take up a collection first thing in the morning to bury the both of you. Blowing all that wind out of your lungs, you'll send yourselves deeper than Cain. Save your air. Tomorrow we'll do all that stuff, if that hurricane that they reported on the radio don't come this way and blow us all up on the mountain." Monson preaching with his well-pronounced pra-pra.

"Hurakán's coming this way. All we heard on the radio was more salsa than fish." Outside the Tropical Junk Shop the nightly tropical sounds were increasing, sharper in the moist nightly darkness. Chirping, howling, hissing, insects that sound buzzardly making their audio, layers on layers. Species must be talking to each other of some content. What business of ours would it be? Some immense star of information filling the scales of their stomachs. Monson got the better of the industrial production; the night was his music, like those nights of hot chocolate and espiritista stories. A jungly moon inside the guitar story of the five senses. Monson, to be further convincing, even found coconut shell cups. Serving ourselves the kenepa juice and rum, we settled back into full compliance with the lunar pull.

"Your grandfather used to drink coffee out of these shells, get up at five in the divine of morning, wipe his dreams from his forehead, start the process to make the coffee. He used to like it black with three spoons of brown sugar, flap, flap, flap, then he'd go stand by the door and watch the forming commotion of the sky. That's how folks were back then. They used to look out into the yonder, decipher the weather from sky and birds, up early to go to the cane fields, their machetes hanging from their waist belts, walk down to the plaza to wait for the truck to pick them up. Whoever wasn't cutting cane was making cigars. Black coffee in the first shadows of morning and zoom into motion. The tabaqueros would be singing and humming by seven. Watch out that by ten they didn't have a stick of rum for the tedious motion of the tobacco roll. Back in 1934 time hardly moved; one moment had to get the other out of bed. But you know everything use to taste better in coconut shells." Monson savoring his second kenepa-and-rum shellful, and we not far behind. A smooth sweet pulp going down dissolving to allow the rising of the hidden alcohol. A tip of fruit that blows up as it drops down the stairs toward the batey of the throat, a radiation coming back up, waving like tall cane over your head in the field. More rum juice as the night centers itself. Less traffic out in the streets. Voices that were coming from distant mountain shelves simmering down. All around us we could feel the Christians going to bed. The old molienda could be heard grinding themselves into finer grain. An occasional rooster boasted of its feats. Chickens formed into ovals asleep on tree branches. The dancing in the plaza now became a clear shuffling of shoes, dresses lifted right above the knees as if to direct the mambos toward further flower, tonight, tonight, perhaps, perhaps, out there somewhere lovers embrace under a tree. Like a stew the night was boiling, a vapor of festive thrills rising to the local mountain crests.

Marifolio in a spell was fidgeting with the shortwave radio, knowing well that the early hours of the morning made more waves available, opened the currency of the sky. He tranced into a rum drum with it. Then Cuba came over a frequency. Had he been mute he would have exploded. "Aha, here it is! Radio Habana, coming in clear and crispy."

He took out the personal headphones so that we all could hear the Benny More big orchestra, the guaguancó from Cuba going to meet the riffs of the local band out in the plaza. He brought the volume up loud, barbarous blows in unison as if the composition were rising in spirals. Maraca to maraca, island to island. "Cuba and Puerto Rico are two wings from the same bird," says the poet. Different Caribbeans come in over the shortwave, depending which way the wind is blowing. Marifolio loses the Cuban station right when the locutor surprises us with a flying penis that has entered his broadcasting studio. Marifolio's fingers on the dial like a safecracker searching for the combination. Next, he stumbles upon Jamaica: "Hey, mon, whatta you wan' us to do? Is dee Saxon man dat comere to fix dee clock? 'Cause you can't fuck wid dee time, mon, you gotta be apropos. Dis Caribbee dat like dee comin' late, British say, na way, dat dee heat fucky yo brain and dee feet reggae, reggae." Bob Marley came on, smoking on the humor of a Kingston DJ. The rum turning pictures of the age of exploration, when the Caribbean was full of floating marauders. They all wanted a piece of mound, saw those green patches stretched as arms, pirates horny for golden fleece from honeyed ass. To think that the Dutch almost took San Juan. Had they been successful, what would it be like? Amsterguaynabo. Goudagüez. San Heineken. Muñoz Rivera Straat. The English from Jamaica cracking up into static, departing from the band. More audio snow till finally a oui-oui of Guadeloupe French, a beautiful sound reaching us from the south. But que disais, del oui oui madame con le monsieur, très bon, con mi de oui con le merci merci too tambien. The Guadeloupe station threw on some U.S. rock and roll and we changed the dial before the beat damaged the junk. "Now I got Miami, listen, Cuban English. Now that woman is beautiful, I can tell from her voice. It's from Key West. From there you can swim to Cuba."

"What I can tell is that she has auburn hair. She'd look Gallician fair if it were not for her Chinese eyes."

"That's a whole lot to pick up from a voice, Monson, or is it the rum you are talking from."

"You're still young. There are signs in life that tell what is coming. You've just got to pay attention, read the fuzzing of the hands, the gestures of the bodies 'stead of them books all the time."

Through the sound waves we could hear some kind of thunder falling on Miami, which soon fell into static, a scattering like black beans in congri, lost with lightning flashes. Marifolio was more in control, smiling along with the vanishing bottle of rum juice, like a NASA scientist scanning the night sky. "Listen, now, we've got a cruise boat that's out there. They're doing the pachanga out in the middle of the sea. You know, they've got everything on those boats now—dentists, saunas, tennis, pizzerias."

"Those crazy berserkos could probably request to see a psychiatrist while they're out there having a good time. Too much good life gives some people stress. Some needle starts to prick them, something starts to talk to them, and they sit around listening. Inside of them something is talking to something else. They sit there watching this quarrel right through to the end. They don't get off it till they start talking out loud to themselves, or go over to a mirror and make out like a famous singer, doing the motions they saw someone do on TV."

"You're just jealous you can't be out there getting some of that stress." Comfort of sea travel goes out to the idea of the Spaniards coming this way, that *Santa María* with no toilets, those rabid dementals shitting over the sides of the boat, butts in full view. And what with the Andalusian saintly sweet vulgarity of vocabulary, in Guanahani they must've killed flowers just with their speech. They shit on *diez* so as to avoid *Dios* and on to chop up the whole celestial court. The Spanish language even on a chance oil spill goes cocky into the cunty regions by precision or indirect reflection.

"You think we could pull Spain in on these wires."

"Now that's further than an iceberg. What! D'you think you're that telescope in Arecibo?" Monson shot back to a head-stuff'd Marifolio.

"At the Arecibo Observatory they're waiting for an alien radio station to pop in with some of their programmed music —Andromeda Guaguancó, Neptune Mambo. What if they do pick up some otherwordly communication, then what are they going to do?"

"Ah, hello, who it is? . . . From where? . . . Oh . . . we'll be right over . . . Wait . . . can you give us directions how to get there?"

"You know what they're going to do after they settle down from jumping back? They're going to commission a study to see if they can decipher the language coming through."

"Young lad, you must be feeling the effects of the rum your grandfather drank. Just a few shells of that rum juice and you've left the planet." Marifolio speaks as he settles back from the shortwave, which he once again has been able to tune in on Radio Habana coming in like clear sunshine as the ether enters the hours of wee. A danzón special is on, Cachao basically walking and making circles through Arcaño y Sus Maravillas, his index fingers lifting the danzón strut further out into the twinkling stars decorating dance shoes.

Monson pours the last of the rum juice into our shells, dancing charangony with all his motions, then he violins: "Come over here, both of you. Listen, I've got a relative, Soraida, married to a minister; the guy is crazy as can be. She weighs 300 pounds and the guy is jealous, gives her a black eye at least twice a year, a jealous Christian. Who knows why, but that's that. So she stopped going to the church. She says, with that mountain plaintain attitude, 'Right to hell it is that he is going. After knowing what's in the pot, you think I'm gonna stick around for dinner. For me, what works is a candle and a glass of water and Santa Marta's image hanging on the wall. They could go down to the church to see each other, or for who knows what they want. I sit down to pray at the white table in my house, and I radiate right there. Let them sing all the songs they want, they can't cover the firmament with their palms.' And like that is how she put it. She goes to these sessions not far from the Arecibo Observatory, and what the espiritistas there are saying is that all the radiation that the radio telescope is attracting is taking possession of the local mediums. People there are getting mental pictures from beyond the craters of Pluto. You know what I'm telling you now. Stuff is coming in but in such a way that it does not go through the telescope once it is drawn into the region. The espiritistas are picking it up on the coast. Those people are dealing with electricity; they are conduits; they start feeling a chill like needles climbing up their arms; next thing it's on their shoulders; then they start to sparkle and snap till they get Xerox copies of stellar dreams, minds lifting all these wayward Milky Way disembodied entities. Soraida says people have burst out speaking in some foreign blah-blah, like merengue tapes in reverse. It's crazy but true. I'm going out there with her some day. Those people from NASA, if they want to know what's happening, that's where they should send their scientists."

"Maybe that telescope some day will pick up Fu Manchu scatting like Mon Rivera from the other side."

"Now I know you're drunk—that electricity is getting to you. Don't go near no water, you'll blow up."

The empty bottle of rum juice was laughing by itself as we divided into early morning particles, walking out into the street to dissolve like sugar in café, to wobble with intent toward the place of sleep. The kenepas must've been from Ponce, that pearl to the south, 'cause it was from that direction that the sound of all entropic creation seemed to be coming. Reaching the house, the moon looked like it was hanging from the avocado tree in the back. In the junk shop a bag of balloons unblown, all 3,000 of them, like everything else, in need of oxygen.

Night alone, the air takes us to the bottom of the Atlantic to witness sights we don't understand, pictures which become cuisine. Naked bodies drenched with mud emerging out of the depths of the ocean. We watch them walk out in the silence of the forms, their hairy animal hands carrying bamboo funnels. They rise out, jump up on land, and jump back into the center of the sea, the bamboos sticking up in the air, with which we presume they are breathing. We strain from the shadows to make out their human torsos covered with fish scales. Just when we focus, they go flying upward, not into the sky, for there is none, but into something else, like a firmament of tree roots hanging down dripping blood-red paint. We see then the beaks of the birdlike faces, the steeple of a Catholic church flying sideways, below "La Tuna," intoning Ave Maria in such a timbre that the harmony affects the landscape, the sea exchanges places with the zenith, above the waves now, salty and fertile with fish. Off to the sides cyclopes are sucking on boneless cod. The clouds are pink handkerchiefs of moisture. The scene goes out to the beach. People you know from town, Doña Prana, her daughter Nilsa, Don Berencho, Efrain, Monson, all of them coming to land pouring from the mouths of fish. The priest of the local church is making love to a neighbor's wife. It must be the interior of night, when the apparatus of the caverns films the hand and the cameras. Fish are now squirming on trees. Is it that disembarking masquerade coming to the chamber of sleep to play its games? Change the channels of the TV so rapidly that each time you focus something else pops up, runs across, ascends, descends, appears in the center, vanishes to the origin of nowhere.

There is that guy who comes to the plaza and stares up into the sky till a second person comes along and imitates him, looking up to see what this other one sees. Next thing you know, there's this crowd out there looking up, a flock of town, and the guy goes: "Shush, it's coming, keep looking. I saw it yesterday two times. Sometimes it comes from that mountain, sometimes it comes from that one, but it eventually comes."

So there's the crowd, lips hanging out, staring into the afternoon sky. Clouds pass, birds pass. They don't even notice the guy leave. The guy now walks down the street, goes to the back door of the local bakery as usual and requests a piece of bread, which one of the bakers hands him. Back out on the street he passes the church, not far from the center of the plaza, where a ball of humans are spellbound staring into the sky. He goes to his cousin's house 'cause he knows she has made the three o'clock coffee; it is time for the caffeine pause. From his cousin's balcony he looks out toward the plaza, drinking his sweet café cup, and turns to her: "Look at that conglomerate of Christians. Has Jesus come from above?" But his cousin knows there's no mind to pay attention to, so she just continues stirring with a big old spoon the pot of red beans that she is making for supper, pig foot, sofrito, that that calabaza sweet as she sings "come in, comino" and pours the garlic adobo.

The episodes change like great rapids. The beings who were in the ocean have disappeared. Now there is no ocean or sky to reflect it. In the interior of an unconscious skull the university turns its lights on. There's Juan Ramón Jiménez giving a lecture. Streaming from his shoulders is a string of flowers rising to exhibit themselves in frames, creating a museum up in space. Walls are up, a labyrinth which can be walked, cuadros hanging on every side. From the poet's hands crystal feminine figurines start to fly. From an impressionist painting land escapes, a river emerges, swells out of its bed, tired of its own cause, of its flow, of all the crab that swims and walks. The feminine floats through the Sophia of the waters to become hands that pick up the curves of the river right out of the territory, wrap it around transparent hips, wet hair like shining asabache. Sweet water entangos through hands. It is a game they play—now it is a scarf, an Areyto of wraparound skirts. A river is—the belt of a mountain. Only loops of light come from the poet's mouth, loops that go out to encircle the ravines where once the rivers' trajecto soared. Now only the memory is there, a sound that occupies. A local promenade for shoeless bones, complete with a sense of touch, for the feet have become wet. The campus vanishes into a fountain pen the size of a telephone pole, a diminishment takes place, shrinking smaller and smaller, a little bit softer now, a little bit softer now, a little bit softer now, a little bit softer now, a little bit softer now. My foot is bigger than the mountain. I can see the local scene, where once the river inked, and now they've built a street in miniature so that it can fit into an envelope as a letter to be sent out toward the luna in the delicate hands of those muses that are smoking cigars now, fingers laden with golden circles, red corals, silver of bracelets, like flying guitars with legs, Segovia musical notes of clay enbroting now on a once again blue sky featuring chocolate stars. Why do I hear now Ismael Rivera the sonero king doing Ecua jere! shouts in a factory of caramels, bonbons that Elena suckles. It rains cocoa in a Bronx of edifices I have never seen, in a Manhattan of cement árboles. Across the screen now enters a screwdriver whose handle is the face of Marifolio, turning and spinning, tightening the screws that are now holding the edges of the mountains. As such, one conjectures with the mist of travel. It makes perfect sense that one should screw those mountains down so that they are not taken away by another invasion of fantasy.

Despite the conditions, a thought flourishes: Register well that the insane don't come out when it rains. Never has a local loco or even an imported one ever been caught in some drenching downpour. They are atmospheric. Way before the brushes paint thickheaded Van Gogh strokes of nubarrónes, across the sky, they receive pictures formed in the nervous rivers of veins which track across their foreheads. The berserk know where you are going and sometimes what you are thinking. You pass in their proximity, and they say: "You left your wife, right?" Whatever could be the case, it sometimes matches with the salsa paste or oregano brujo brewing in your head. On you go past the red signal that struck like a cement wall, toward the green "go" signal, walking till you pass again, this time by a different nut that screws: "At home you've got the beans going." That's the end of that crackpot. Or right through the bodega of life, where a woman had been shopping around: "Get rid of that man. You could do better and he could do worse." Or someone just singsongs out in the most thoughtless of places: "If she puts him to dance, he'll put her to cook."

Even the insane have normal dreams, like Yaye who fashioned his brain at his feet, went into a footage cha-cha-chá that he left a little street and galloped into the maya, that to this day he hasn't been seen. They've heard he's in Río Piedras marching up and down the university campus even though he's not registered, just there parading for the vision, big attaché case that he carries around containing a Mexican wrestling magazine featuring an interview with the great masked Santos, a screwdriver, a pair of pliers, the laminated album cover of El Gallito de Manatí's first recording folded in half, brown paper bags covered with the scribblings of songs, half a pint of Palo Viejo rum, and about twenty pencils, half of which are pointless.

Night, the underground subway heading to the forest, El Barrio of tricksters and other zoology. We could say a wondering of explosive firecrackers, siquitraquis that can even or roundly detonate twenty floors above or below your bed, where life unrolls within a portion of the calendario as you are thrown there with the lid closed. What are the numbers in the square boxes of the weekdays? Tonight they melt like ice cream cones of frambuesas to the delight of al-Andaluz children crossing with their parents upon the backs of camels through the streets and gardens of Cordova. In the darkness of the tunnels, the iron horse of time can be put on fast forward or pushed into rewind. We could stop in the cold blocks of November, like the fingers of the dead painting the tombs bone white, picnic there as a portable radio plays dusty Trio Vegabajeño. And in that caserío of bones, there is now, to look at it afresh, a wonderful view off to a valley that then pimples mountains on the other side, making a rich performance for even the poor of the Rico soul, loose with the freedom of an eye drop. A gathering there of cement crosses, Christs, Virgins, and Saints in stoned positions taking heat for generations. Monumentals, tombstown, a city of marble rectangles where nothing else could fit, so that extensions of wall drawers have been installed for future filing. Watch out that at the ancestral banquet one does not confront a family relation through the veil of particulars, blaming each other for the lack of visits, a kind of fiasco amidst the dead who are giggling. Then they want to rewind the tape of time missed(t) out on, to re-create all that gone duration, right in an instant of loaded euphoria. So it's right after the cemetery that they all go to visit after so many suns and sons. The family jumps with such such that they can't find what else to give you. They take off your shoes and bring you soft slippers, locate the fan to angle you some righteous breeze, that send Joseito, who is now old enough to drive, to the Cash and Carry y Qué for a case of beer. The sound of those aluminum cans popping open, people blaming the moisture for its vanishment when they down it in some three and a half gulps. Was it Isodoro or Remijio that intoned,

"Wait a minute, send for the guitar." A guiro gets an itch that has to be scratched. Finally the tribe gives in, killing the pig that's been grunting about. That's the certain evidence that the visit will go into the next day, staying over thrown wherever. A feast the neighbors will also taste, a stretch of meat down the sierra, flying plates, nine-year-olds tumbling down reddish dirt. "Here sends Aunt Luz." All that as a result of polishing family bone, instant flash Kodaks that visit the remote corners of an eyeball in frenzy in the most snoring of midnights.

Broad panoramas that circulate back to those half-human creatures blasting out of the water, from all mythologies, crisscrossing all points 'cause to these islands who hasn't come to piss. What happened to the bird heads with weightlifter torsos. The rivers becoming skirts and scarves, blue and yellow gold-filled Indian saris, or a balcony of square tiles of Egyptian iconography leading to one room after another, endlessly in and out of apartments looking out on fecund gardens. Where what it is is a Cemi of shapes, magnified island orchids, striking students of all the forms with such a fever that they went videotaping all species of fruits sliced in half, taking prints to the Italians, to the Iraquis, to the Persian architects who made interior walkways in Iran for possible new decorations. Without effort the night enters the epoch when let's say book covers were like the ornamentations of mosque entrances, trancing through the twilight below the coconut palms that are the first to wake in the mornings and go for walks, vision looking for a perfect moor to suspend the Ignerian sofa, spreading the pages of a book so that just the odor is enough, the way Rubén Darío read just by touching and sniffing, the French text smoking in his hands like the rising fragrance of a just opened virginal nacatamal. Awake in dreams are centipedes that stroll in image sandals passing at 100 feet from phonetic soup, predawns as always to assist in the transfer of the invisible into the light of day, a constant flipping over, turning around. What in the day you might recall of the night story, what you thought was just a mambo tango of meaningless susurration, drum drone splatter. It all stays 'cause no Florida water or Indian head hanging with seven hatchets could wipe out the grime of historical gossip from balcony tiles. Those geometric squares are ears swallowing what walks upon them.

That's the night of the realms and their divisions, the glitter of what is hidden in the daylight of junk. Tons of it you must calculate is out there. All those old cameras longing to capture just one more appearance, that they don't dehydrate on this island of so many pupils centering premonitions of the malicious eye. What if the vibes are such that even within a dream a broken TV falls again, the masses turning it on like a cuckoo clock to watch their favorite nothing. To be assaulted by the programmed concerns of bankrupt layouts. The melody of dramatic soap operas—novelas (I've never seen a naked lady taking a bath with Maja soap swinging hip and lip in soprano doing the opera *Orfeo* of Claudio Monteverdi on any of those soap dramas) unfolding nonexistent upper-class entanglements: ah Lorenzo, the son of the hacienda patriarch, has fallen in love with the maid—dadarata—that she's a mestiza—tatarata—that she's india and red brown—lala—that she's African and brilliant—before the car accident and the hospital room scene with someone bandaged like a mummy—the betrayals building—who is gonna go with who. Spare us from such malfunctioning tubes working like new within a dream. Might be that while you're in the ooze of Zs they're filming in Caracas, perhaps Miami, or infinite Mexico City, new chapters. And the actors, where do they find them? Seems like on the day of filming they just stand out on the street outside the television studios and bark at people chancing by, calling them over: "Say, you. You wanna be in." They uplift the B rating, taking a hike further up the alphabet, right through the DDT to the zone of sleeping Zs for Zombies.

Old footage shows up between the posts, under the transparency of the mosquito net, which is no deterrent for Dracula coming to suck you in your dream. Canisters of black-and-white film portraying people walking across wooden boards thrown over marshlands carrying large Sultana cracker canisters full of water. Crowds turn up a street where the dreamer sees himself walking with his young mother amidst the multitude, her long skirt flapping like a flag in the aerial whirl. To a four-year-old child an ox walking through the central street of the town appears as a dragon, a lubberly hippopotamatic creature looking like someone cut a chunk of mountain and inserted legs. Deeper in the archives the town turns from wood to homes of palms and rocks. An Yjuana walks down to a steaming surface, cognac asleep in the abdomen, the rum thyroid, when there were no roads going toward Urugutun, the language there: ovaries and testicles, a cave of motionless bats, a still life painter's oasis. The final films were sent up from the cellar, old wine that the cyclops didn't drink, nothing, just rocks breathing a red lava that invented copulation. At such low lands the sheets come off the mattress, face and feet have exchanged positions. A tropical roach hitting the screen can get you up in the middle of nowhere. (That time a tourist asked for directions when out of nowhere a roach lands on the guy's polo shirt, nice Bostonian. Townspeople jumped there, enthusiastic to help him find the fastest route out of the Urugutun he fell into by accident, somehow he made it to that single road in and out of town which is not on any tourist map. But what happens, he scoped the size of the creature and reacted jerkily [the motions, not the person], started moving back hitting it off the fibers of his shirt and, panicky, dashing toward his car yelling, "Jesus—holy shit—wait!" Slapping it off while he jumped into the car real quick, the car which he had left turned on while he asked for directions—but things happen and he must've by nervous flash floored the gas pedal—still recuperating from the shock of that roach. Pueblo people bad-mouthing the English, trying to say, "Mister-nosing happening"—that stupid ring of voice which assumes anyone from the outside is a teacher—"Mister" as the car with the man in it shot down the short street which immediately became the edge of town and a ravine drop. Down he went, the stranger who just seconds earlier was friendly and more than welcomed—Samuel the Spider had already fetched him a beer bestowed by the cafetin owner—in a matter of forty seconds, half the town was down there making sure the guy was alright. The car had been stopped by a plantain plant from further law of gravity, not far from the cement edge, so that we produced rope and got him out of there. [The guy went bananas.] The car okay, the man composed, he settled down to have his beer, talk and joke back in the cafetin. His name was Marty. He asked after he was reoriented and ready to go: "Jesus Christ, what was that?" And the crowd, having anticipated the question, said it was a condemned bat, yeah, a schizoid blind bat that always comes out in the day puzzling the hell out of people. And he left with that—'cause why tell him the truth.)

Still, the sun is not out, and in the rational of a turn in bed the barking of a pack of dogs stalking the deserted streets climbs to the level of the pillows, dogs howling like wolves. Is it once again those twenty dogs after that one bitch? It then takes a regression down to cats with the next toss doing their life-to-death courting fights, piercing the petals of the night till no more do you hear their penetration. Is it that time of night when all conception is crossing over into the act, the whole neighborhood locked in lust? Men and women who live find each other's spots. Between three and six in the morning, the sugar in the coffee is being stirred, the spoon scraping the bottom circling there. Why? 'Cause the sugar is there. When? When the coffee is hot. Why? 'Cause the night is black and the milk is boiling. Is it not, then, within that zone of time when cocks sing in simalcas? Could be the moon has turned into a comb, a fine and expensive one made of jade. It is grooming all fur, brushing here, stroking there. An undercurrent communion between cock and cock. Roosters up singing right in Spanish cacaracu, before any sight or thought of the lamp, the sun rising on their feathers. They sing to take inventory, a call to the living, to clean their beaks, one supposes. Up in that mountain cacoling—ah—cooocooorucooo.

Arrows of light spraying through the blinds, the rising of the hot bread at the bakery. Someone with early nostalgia Trio Mayarí's the bed frame. The talk of junk rises early. It is Marifolio out there with some industrial hangover. Someone was passing, and from my bed I could hear the exchange.

"I can't get the wires of the radio separated from the wires of the fan."

"That's how good the rumba was last night. There was so much heat that it went looking for the fan to cool off."

"The mother that gave you birth."

Everything that belonged to me was up and awake, except my eyes, which were glued shut. Inside the sockets, my eyeballs were two dried fruit pits. The night, what was that?

PRIMEROS SONIDOS

La Hamaca

Las antiguas culturas de las
Antillas
Inventaron el mejor
Aparato
Para hacer el amor:
La Hamaca.

Cuando los otros centros
De cultura
Estaban produciendo
Filósofos,
Telescopios,
Pirámides,
Y el hombre moderno
Seguio inventando
Radios y televisiónes,
La bomba nuclear,
El agente orange,
Tinta amarilla número tres,
El hamburger—la pizza—

Los ingenieros Tainos
Se dedicaron a lo basico—
Estudiando la anatomía
Y los ritmos del cuerpo
La altura de su ciencia
Declaro:
Pase lo que pase
Esto nunca pasara de estilo,
En la hamaca se puede
Uno ir hasta el hueso.

Poema Chicano

Los Angeles de mi Chihuahua Mamá
Su carrucho de burgundy.
Ciudad que empieza y no acaba
Hay más calles que estrellas.
José Montoya poeta de Sacras-Califas,
El del Royal Chicano Air Force—
El del Highway 99
El higuey—
El de aguellas ese
De la balada ranchera
Lo dijo bien:
"Los Angeles es un desmadre, una pinche perdida allí y de
    lleva la chingada."

Rucas de amanecer-mole poblano-chile verde besos
La china poblana-sarape panties-jalapeño miradas
Las Lupitas que salsita down Pico Avenue
Que crucigrama con Sunset Boulevard—
Más largo que Cuba,
Sus malinche lenguas de la poesía
El guachupín Cortez padre de las voladas
Bilingües.

L.A. del cielo químico
Se vive en el carro—
Se pasan paredes de murales aztecas
Mascaras de Chichimecas ojos
Cachetes yaquis enchinaos
Harina de maíz en metate de colores
Sueños de mescal—por sorpresas
De Olivera Street—ciudad en medio

De un desierto.
Maravilla Housing Projects
Vatos locos
Pandilleros, cocos pelaos
Tatuajes como is fueran
Lienzos para Frida Kahlo.
Homegirls rucas
Bonitas doncellas con el
Tatuaje de la cruz azul
En sus manos—
Hablan palomitas de calo
Al lado de carruchos
Pintados como is fuesen
Pirámides—
Olor de carnitas y frijoles
Bajan en alas de aguilas.
Desde las ventanas
El acappella de los oldies
El Little Joe y la Familia.

Ahora en esta antillana isla
Me recuerdo tus panes dulces—
Y tus picantes Serranos.
Aquel East Los
Infinito Barrio
Echo Park
Frogtown
El Mercado
Como is estuvieses en México
Grande como liga de fútbol
Mariachi por todo aire—
Braceros con sus botas de cuero

Tequilasos de Simón ese,
Bigotes que llegavan a la frontera—
Su español volado tejiendo
Por aquéllos otros Chicanos
Más pachucados pochos
Creando un tráfico de polka
Y emplumado mescalito hip-hop
Por todo el San Bernardino.

Órale, pues—
A la chingada el español
Y el inglés:
"Hey vato, where's Chuey ese."
"Está en la chante con su ruca, trais fralo, dame trola.
Buena yeska—Tijuana mamá—tus ojos llegan a Jalisco,
Jalisqueate ya."
Virgen Guadalupeña—Ponte trucha
Por todo Aztlán
Estrella Mística.

La Virgen como tatuaje
En la espalda de aquél
Que le dicen el Chino—
El que era pinto
Allá en Soledad
También en San Quin—
El más chingón
Carnal del Fredy Mejias
De Santa Ana
Llegava como la breeza.
Se conocieron en la pinta,
Estaba todo el East Side

Y el Valley también—
Hijos de Pachucos
Generaciónes de low riders
Esa vena que se va por Arizona
En el Interstate 10
Y llega a Albuquerque
Nuevo México—
Las Sandia Mountains
Huevos rancheros
Las Cruces
Llano Quemado—
Ojos Caliente
El Río Grande gorge
Mirar pa abajo
Es ver el infierno—
Esos Páramos de Juan Rulfo
En el norte
Mariachi y turquesa
Pueblo Taos ancestro collares—
Huercas con ojos de pura plata
Llenos del firmamente Oaxaca
Como oyen todo el metote
Las sultanas—
Oigo los caracoles danzante
De Andres Segura—
La fragancia del copal
El orale pues—los híjoles
Descienden por la montaña
Borincana de Jagueyes.

El Californow de retratos
Los zoot suits
Sombreros de aquéllas

Estas qualifi—
Saludos Juan Felipe Herrera
". . . show me the way to San Jose"
Y tus cantos de paya papaya va paya.
Alejandro Murguia y las perdidas
Que nos dimos buscando a la tamalera
Callejera y la tortillera casera—
Y el Alurista que se inventó Aztlán
De la mitología—
Como cruzavamos la frontera—
Empezavamos en Chicano Park / San Diego
Y llegabamos pistiando hasta Ensenada
Casi sin feria
Donde en la playa
Taquitos de sesos y madres—
Aquél viejo que dijo:
"Ponle limon a todo para evitar
la cruda de éstas son las mañanitas."

Ah, California, mi segundo país
Hoy suenas con el Suavecito de Malo
Y el jingo pop de Santana.
Y los bellos terremotos
Porque allí hasta la misma
Tierra bailaba.
California el poppy de oro,
Rascacielos de redwoods
Califorica
Californow
Califas
c/s
Con Safos.

Yo No Digo Que Esto No Es Importante

El radio telescopio radar de Arecibo
Esperando la música, del infinito
En la visual pantalla del cálculos
De los años de luz—
Si antes los Taínos
Soñaban desde las cavernas
Los rincones del cielo
Archivados en los árboles de Ceiba
En la orilla del río,
Y en África la tribu Dogan
Tenía la estrella Sirius
En la retina de sus ojos cerrados
Sin tener ni sequiera una lupa.

Es por su presencia
Arquitectónica de embelecos
Que hoy sabemos
Que el planeta Mercurio no
Gira a la velocidad
Anterior cientificada—
Con este descubrimiento ya yo
Me siento mejor.

Más cerca y sin amplificación
Está el hecho que la última tormenta
Nos dejo sin café—
Y bicho sea de paso
El vuelo de una mosca
En las afueras de un barrio
De Abidjan África

Puede causar ciertas reacciónes
En el aire
        Para así contribuir
A la formación en la atmósfera
De condiciones favorables
Como para que nazcan sistemas
Tropicales—
Que sigue el zumbeo hacia
Grandes depresiones
Que ni un siquitrac puede curar.
Como la manzanita
Torbellino tormenta de Hortense
Pasar una noche estancada—
Incómoda y horrible
Tal vez de pesadillas
Y amanecer como Hurakán.

Esc Arecibeño ojo cosmológico—
Costo 40 millones de dólares
Para construir—
Hay que añadirle los costos anuales
De operaciones desde el 1963—
Y ahora le van a meter 30 millones más
Para mejorar su puntería.
Ese show sí que está caro.

Maginate que por esos cables
Salga una entidad
Reclamando ser el cacique Arecibo
Pidiendo que le regresen
El nombre Abacoa al Río Grande
Todo esto en sonido maracanet

Y no estas letras alfas
Despues con beta lenguatiaje
Salivoso griego románticos
Enfenecidos impulsos cadizcos—
Una arawakania eléctrica
Desde piedras retratos.
Comprendo la necesidad
De saber la distancia
De algún asteroide borracho.
Empujar con el dedo un botón
En la costa norte Puerto Rico
Para que desde las antenas
Parta una melodia a penetrar
Zonas de nubes interestelares
Desde el Caribe al carajo
Para hacerle entrevistas
A las estrellas nacientes
Que se visten de nuevas moléculas
Camisas de brillo—
Sin saber que alguien
Las liga
Poniendose la nueva ropa de luz.

Si fuesen boleristas—
Pudieran ver las estrellas
Caídas en las miradas ardientes.

Después de todas las ilusiones
Sonando por el aire:
¿De qué nos agarramos?
Los estudios para confirmar
A Einstein:

Lo grave de la gravedad
Donde no van ni los sueños
Cualquier objeto rompe
El deseo del espacio
Y se chupa todo lo que se mueve.

En 33 años de ese plato Arecibeño
(Servirá para servirle a los
Cíclopes is aparecen un asopao
De gandules)
Arte de escultura—
Alexander Calder en su mejor momento,
Desde el principio hasta el cabo
No les ha llegado
Un singular mensaje
Ni invitación a algún
Baile extraterrestre
(Que se sepa).

Ah,
Si pudiéramos manifester
El olor a guayaba madura
En su punto
Por las 5.9 billones de millas
De un año de luz.

Desde este radar
Se está calculando
A que velocidad
Se están alejando
Las galaxias de la Tierra—
Por si no sabías

Que éstas están huyendo
A todo este
TRAQUETEO.
Un planeta con tanto
Dinero
Y no podemos comprar
Otra luna:
Jupiter tiene trece.

Dicen que tiene un oscuro y profundo
Interior subterráneo—
Si los mensajes que mandan pa fuera
Llegan en años de luz—
Imaginense la repuesta
Oye—
No se podría mientras tanto
Usarlo para madurar aguacates.

Preparaciones para el Pasado

Dicen algunos que se fue todo el mundo—
Cabeza a pies—retratos y maletas
Hacía el polyester norte—
Que también era clima pa abajo.
Sin saber mi familia se fue en noviembre—
Aterrizando en medio de una tormenta nieve
De aquéllas de los cincuentas.
Se puede decir que llegamos
Desnudos
Envueltos en hojas de guineo
Con unas maletas que se compraron
En la Esquina Famosa
Al cruzar la calle de la plaza.

Cemento y hierro
Borrando olor a madera vieja
A vientos con frutas,
Al pan caliente de un tal Colorao
Y que de los Hernández
De Aguas Buenas panadería.
Los ladrillos
Como pasteles rectangulares
Eliminando el chocolate de los
Árboles.

No se sabía ni por que nos fuimos—
O sería yo
Que en el sal pa fuera
De los cinco años no tenía
Ni son ni ton por no decir

Mente analítica—
Todo era como sensación y apetito
Luz y altura
Velocidad
Cosas nuevas para comer,
Dulces no gofios
Las botellas no servían
Para pirulí.

Nombres ya sonidos
Recordados vía memoria
Reciente historia
Caras desaparecidas:
Como Paco El Chácaro
Martillando herraduras
A caballos pintados
Como dinausaros
En el retrato con
Trasfondo de casa
Verde o amarilla
No sé is fue azul
De madera
O is fue ya blanca de cemento.

Cual distancia tenía
La plaza
Pienso al mirar el cielo gris
Más chiquito el cielo
Aún más grande el país—
Eran cinco cuadras
O eran dos—
Patronales fiestas

Cohetes se arriman
Conmigo al río
Cerca de Peter Stuyvesant
Luces en la oscuridad
De la perdida
Interior cueva
Donde vivía y que un Mago
Y varios desaparecieron
Con sus retos de Machismo
Borracho
A ver quién iba más profundo.
Fue algo oido
Por eso de la oreja—
No sé is en calle Muñoz Rivera
O is en la 101
Cuál era la diferencia—
Colmado que se fue a bodega.
Será verdad que nunca
Salieron de las cavernas
Del callejón sin salida.

Nombres rurales en lo urbano—
Parra y algo de San Felipe
Ciriaco, Fesnomelina, Epifanio
Triburcio de qué?
O fueron todos tormentas
Pensaba yo junto con las
Nuevas palabras
Que explotaban
Por la metropolis—
Mirándolas sin saberlas
Desde la nueva transparencia

De cristal ventana
Con vistas de la geometría
De cemento.

De noche
Después de eternos revuelcos
Buscando el ladito para dormir
Los primeros sueños
Menos coquí sonidos
Menos sonidos de coquís
Que desde vientre se oían.

La nieve como sabana tendida
En las calles
Creando un silencio de diccionario.
Veranos bocinas subiendo
Desde avenidas
Que nunca acababan—
Infinita brea.
Andando o corriendo
Sobre ellas
Veía al colmado de Don Pino
Me veía yo mismo
Pantalones cortos
Arrimarme al mostrador
Pedir tres centavos de tabaco
De masticar
En mandado que estaba
Para mi abuela negra
Para mi abuela india
Para mi abuela que fumaba.

Paloma que volaba
Ya no guaraguao—
Ni gallinas que se escondían
Detrás escaleras de mármol
Ni pío pío que entendían
Los nuevos gallos en el City.
Volando como el aire
Las alas de la niñez
Lo mismo monte
Que fire escape
Llegar al manantial nevera
Y sentir el agua desde
La boca a los pies—
Transparente sensación
Conectando a uno de hueso a piel—
Como Donald Duck en una
Comiquita
Cuando bebía tinta
Se ponía azul.

Pesadillas
Que uno juraba
Que habían vacas
En el nuevo apartamento
Que era viejo—
O siempre la posibilidad
De enmaletados alacranes
Que volaban gratis
Brincar al medio de la
Carpeta la de linoleum,
Gritería y corre y corre
A punto de tumbar

El cisne de un espejo
Enganchado en pared color
De rosa—
Bajo sofa anaranjado
En plástico cubierto.

Todavía fresco como pan
En la mente caliente
La vez que tíos alegres
Entraban pal subway
Guitarras en manos
En época de navidad
Sin saber
Que se tenía que pagar—
Y el hombre de atrás
La casita les grita:
"Hey, hey, token."
Y los jíbaros rompieron
En un seis cagüeño—
Como el hombre dijo "token"—
Y tuvo que llegar los guardias
Para hacerlos parar y pagar.

Y luego la pérdida
De los padres
Buscando sin saber
Una parada Bushwick
Que no existía—
Preguntando direcciones
En inglés mal hablado
Y peor entendido.
Como botellas

Que se caen y se hacen
Vidrio era el nuevo
Lenguaje sonido.

De siete años me eliminaron
Pa la escuela
Lleno de fragmentos
De dos idiomas
Un revoltillo de berenjena
Un cuadro de Picasso borracho
Pintado con sonido
En el lienzo del aire—
Speek entonces english
Fue lo primero que oí
Era un speak de hablar
Que se convirtió en spic.

Se vacío la isla
Porque todos Po'rican allí—
Alegría tropical sobre:
"See Jane run,
See Dick and Jane play,
Come see, said Dick,
Run, Jane, run . . ."
Y sobre todo por las
Mañanas el himno nacional
El cual nunca aprendimos
En dicción total
Por cual nos metimos
En problemas un grupito
Pos cuando el himno
Dice: "Oh say can you see"

Nosotros oíamos:
"José, can you see"
Y riendo señalábamos
A los dos Josés en la clase—
Al principal tuvimos que ir,
Llamaron a nuestras
Madres para darles la queja
En inglés—
El cual ellas todavía
Amapolas, pomarosas
Y hierbas de campos
Menos sabían—
Pero el día que llegaron
Ellas lo más atentas
Al ramillete de sonidos
Que brotaba—
Movían las cabezas
Para como quien dice,
Una valiente Mayagüezana
Decía: "Yeah, yeah, yeah"
Repetidamente.

Regresando a casas de viandas lunas—
Roperos con memoria
De fragancia patcholi
Caos de tristeza
Penas del olvido
Preso en bolero guitarras—
Versos de amores perdidos
Voces de antaño resonaban
Por los emplastos de las paredes
Del Hallway—

Se intercambiaban con la almuada—
En un sueño de niñez
Pequeñas manos abrazaban
La canción—
Al ver que una montaña
Llamada el pasado
Se hacía chiquita
En la distancia de la fantasía—
Se iba—más chiquita
Tan pequeña que apareció
En las manos
Brillante como un
Juguete.

Pronóstico: Arte

Si quieres ir al museo,
Tira tus ojos al cielo.
El pintor es el viento—
La brisa como la brocha
Dibujando nubes de yuca
Blanca y la sábana en
Azul marino de trasfondo.
Voz del aire
Que abre como alfombras
Persas
Por encima de los montes
Platanales contra la ley de gravedad
Aspirando a irse de la tierra—
Las flores prostitutas de la luz
Brican hacia
Los círculos del nada.
El merengue bien batido
Nubes como leche derramada
Cielo dulce y azul.
Celeste tropical:
Estudios y equipo
El tiempo jamás podrán pronosticar.
Anarquía de niños al pintar
Sale agua del mismo sol.
Los dibujos de los navajos
El camino de les estrellas.
En la pantalla inmensa
Nubes como las columnas
De los romanos—
Las pirámides de Tenochtitlán

Pintados en el cenit.
Nalgas como ballenas blancas
Se hacen y se desbailan en humo—
Sabrosas gordas
De las cual el pueblo grita:
"Pide que hay."
Reposan para que las pinte Botero
Desde Colombia.
El aguacero se anuncia con
Un ballet de Golondrinas—
Sale Van Gogh maniático
A pintar el mar
Igual que comen
Los holandeses
En los cuadros de Rembrandt
Pa encima sobre el costal.
Infinita piedra cristal de turquesa
Por donde el marinero Miró
Saca a los peces a respirar aire
Mientras el cielo se llena
De elefantes sabios
Y mascaras de caracoles.
Abajo:
PlenaRumbaMerengue
Puerto Rico—Cuba—Santo Domingo:
En película el primer mestizaje
Vivo y en acción,
Pueblos encadenados en el baile,
Sudor que es música y artesanía.
Imagen que a sobrevivido
Una locura de Dalí.
Nuevo aire del cielo

Donde Juan Ramón Jiménez
Enganchó sus lentes—
Las frutas fragmentadas
De Wilfredo Lam
Árboles mariposas, Panorama
La brocha que pinta bamboos
En papel de arroz
De la esencia China como
Rocío de Aibonito en seda.
Los vapores de la Tequila
Que se fue para Aztlán
Salen de los pedazos de
Yucatán que pasan por los altos.
Las manos Dogan de Cardenas:
Piedra Negra
Señalando hacia la estrella Sirius
Vista por sus manos sin telescopio,
Un azul oscuro—húmedo total
Caribeño cielo—
Cada momento otro ritmo.
Arte celeste
Para bautizar la ceremonia.

Poema Homenaje a Julita en Su Cumpleaños 99: Un Siglo de Presencia

Hoy Julita nos brinda un siglo de presencia
Pues la persona es concebida en una mirada—
Luego los nueve meses navegando en el mar—
Cien años de soledad—
Cien años de solidaridad—
Cien años de sol—
Cien años de sol en campo—
Cien años de árbol de tantas frutas—
Cien años de luna—
Y de café colao—
Negro y en tránsito hacia el tabaquero
Que con sus dedos enrolaba los boleros
De humo y del pasado—
1897
En Washington estaba el Presidente McKinley—
Planificando como coger a Cuba y a Puerto Rico
En el Caribe
Y en el 1889
Pasamos de las manos de los españoles
A los americanos—
Y el jíbaro en la distancia
Bailando sus garabatos
Cantando sus cadenas que en Aguas Buenas
Habían más de cien.
En un balcón del Pueblo
Jugaba y sonreía una niña
Sin saber que nos ocupaban
Los Marinos Americanos—
Del Café entramos al Tabaco—

A despalillar hojas se fueron las mujeres—
Cantando y hablando
Para mandar cigarros a Chicago—

Desde el río donde se lavaba la ropa,
La luna era más de plata
Con más memoria de su otro nombre
En los labios de nuestra sombra Taína
Para quien ese satélite era símbolo de hombre—
Pues el sol era la diosa hembra de brillante oro—
Julita sabe que aquí mandaban las mujeres,
Cacicas que abrazaban todo el horizonte,
Todos salimos bailando de las cuevas—
A las manos de las comadronas.

Julita sabe que el río estaba mas fecundo—
Las orquídeas en el bordado de los trajes
Que eran más largos—más amarillos y más blancos
Sobre la voz del bolero—
Nocturnas serenatas—
Las señoras hablaban con sus abanicos
Alfabetos en el aire que eran mensajes precisos—

Vivió la epoca de las canciones
Que para nosotros son las de ayer
Tejido de las noches de quinque,
Luz y sombra—
Vibrando en el aire las cuerdas
De la Bordonia de Secundino Merced—
Instrumento moro del desierto Sahara
Caminando como un camello por el seis chorriao

El sol que está en sus ojos
Vieron las casas de madera transformarse en cemento—
Los caserónes de la plaza y la iglesia colonial
Por ser española—
La que hoy parece un terminal de guaguas de California—
Vió las frescas lomas llenas de amapolas
Y los últimos bohíos que acariciaron las montañas.
Por la costa del norte abrazaba el ferrocarril.

Si las miradas se conviertieran en objetos de la
Historia se llenaría el aire de gofio y planchas pesadas—
Tejido de tapetes y colchas hechas a mano,
Gigantescos pilones, molinillos para hacer harina de café.
Aroma que abría paso por un Barrio de Madera—
Barrio con nombre de fruta nativa.
Por un enorme radio Emerson
Salían las campanitas de Rafeal Hernández
Con El Cuarteto Victoria—
Por la calle viéramos pasar un camión cargando—
Largas varillas de caña—
Y más picada que las que se caían al piso
Observaríamos a mi abuelo Julio El Bohemio
En la esquina de su tango.

Julita cambió la lámpara por la bombilla,
La fogata por la estufa,
La agricultura desapareció en la industria
Fue testigo de las épocas—
En esa perseverancia encontramos los pasos perdidos.
Lo que vieron sus ojos lo sentimos
En las caricias de sus manos.

Hoy esta Tribu te brinda este
Homenaje—
Por ese siglo que nos has brindado
Que se convierte en un areyto
Al hacer un circulo completo
Y repetir con perseverancia de tradición
Por hacernos más unidos
Y más Pueblo
Más familia y mas puertorriqueños:
Hoy Julita nos brinda un siglo
De presencia.

      —Aguas Buenas, Puerto Rico
        Abril 25, 1996

Loísaida

Cómo fue que las montañas desaparecieron,
En las maletas las frutas de su memoria,
Aquel sonido amarrado en yuntas de pasteles
Cubierto con papel de aluminio
La fragancia del Caribe en los puertos de la tecnología,
El polyester nuevo de las guayaberas
En norteñas ciudades de Van Huesone.
Ciudad donde el tiempo no tiene son-risa
Las tres son las tres
No hay ñaqui ni octavitas
Judíos bajo la regla anglo
Perdieron su orientación
Maestros de escuela
Hablaban sin mover los brazos
Cabezas inmóviles
Como clavos en cemento,
Eran policías de los labios
En los salones de las escuelas tenían una ley
Que no se podía hablar español,
Detrás de los ladrillos los cantos de pueblos perdidos,
El sofrito emigró sin el sol—
Pitirre de fire escape—
Las montañas en los ojos de ayer—
Llegamos desde otro tiempo—
Era noviembre
Le tendremos que decir a T. S. Eliot
Que abril no es el mes más cruel,
Sin abrigos entramos por la puerta industrial
Casi desnudos volando por el aire sin soñar.

Las montañas estaban en los retratos,
Las ventanas que eran de madera ahora
Con vista hacía los plátanos—
Antenas del Empire State Building
El edificio Chrysler como una varilla para lechón,
Desde los altos techos salían palomas en pandillas
A volar libres sobre el aire contaminado con progreso.

En Loisaida ya los ladrillos estaban cansados,
El peso de los judíos los debilitó,
Los irlandeses en la Tercera Avenida
Ya los habían quemado—
Barrio de judíos que escaparon hornos y fuegos,
Por las paredes
Se oían los gritos de los campos de concentración,
Había rotulos con letreros hebreos que parecían ganchos
De pescar,
Locos y locas viejos recientes escupidos
De una Europa medieval andando con sus
Zapatos del viejo mundo
El sonido de bombardeos como película en sus nervios

Los veíamos al ellos mirarnos a nosotros,
Un lenguaje para sobrevivir,
De largos caminos entre los campos y las ciudades,
Señoras polacas que caminaban como ancianas
De Aibonito con los mismos velos negros
Hacía la misma iglesia católica.
Campesinos del mundo caídos como frutas
Maduras de sus árboles nativos.

Antes de los proyectos los edificios llegaban

Hasta el río
El Río Este
Muelles y apartamentos de marinos mercantes,
Putas irlandesas y judías
Casas de juego—
Por la Tercera Avenida los teatros burlescos—
El Bajo Manhattan fue hecho para trabajadores
Y ganguistas
Los sueños eran números
Todo el carbón que entraba a la "boiler"
Buscaba maneras de salir del bajo mundo—
Este sal is puedes
El culo de Manhattan—
La puerta trasera de la ciudad
Todo llegaba ilegal
Equipo y ropa,
Colchas y platos,
Importados de la Quinta Avenida,
Las calles eran fiestas de andar
Como tránsito de hormigas.
Por las ventanas abiertas
La gente parecía salir de las paredes—
Sin tantos teléfonos los gritos
Eran de radio bemba—
Más Po'ricans enflorecían
Avenida pachanga música
Como is los ladrillos fuesen bocinas—

Allá por las delicatessens famosas de los
Judíos Katzes y Ratners
Hacían unos sandwiches que no cabían
Ni por la boca abierta de un hipopótamo

Pasaban los jóvenes callejeros
Con sus colores de gangas
Para hacerse mostaza
Por calles que se perdían
Bajo de sus pies—

Vamos a decir una esquina se prende en fuego—
Porque hay guitarra y safacón que se coge pa tambor—
Y como todavía estaba llegando gente desde el sol
Se entonaba un a zoom zoom baba—é de canción
Con botella y pote el guaguancó
Que is era viernes seguía hasta las dos.
Para dónde se fue el cantar de los gallos—
Dicen que los que vinieron maduros ya tenían su reloj—
En la oscuridad fría ya estaban de pie
Escuchando a radio WADO colando Café Bustelo
El locutor Tirado de Guayama repartiendo
Las condiciones del tiempo en la isla:
Ochenta y soleado
Para mejor mirar por las ventanas
A los montes de nieve
Antes de salir a pelear con las calles.

Tal vez al abrir el buzón hay una amapola
Una carta con sentido de mamey
Un pitirre en un sobre cantando.

Los primeros besos
No eran al lado del río cerca de árboles de pomarosas
Y bambúas
El romance conducía hacía el roofo,

Para ver galaxias de luces
Enredos de dedos y pelo—
Como calefacción en el hallway rodeados de mármol

Cómo fue que desaparecieron las montañas
En murales del sueño pintadas—
Se convirtieron en cuentos para pasar el frío.
El inglés pasó por ellas como un río
Doblando los acentos de monte adrentro—
El que se fue no es el que llegó
Y lo que dejó ya no está.

Por dónde pérdidas andan las montañas,
Se fueron conmigo a bailar en el Bronx,
Solamente son palabras en mi corazón,
Son cucubanos de letras las que me alumbran a mí
Ceiba con raíces en el subway
Yagrumo en Rockefeller Center
Por las calles la música de Mayarí
Rafael con su guitarra sentado en las
Escaleras de la 116—
Teatro Puerto Rico Daniel Santos
Piña en los escenarios de Broadway
El Río Hudson ya casi es Maví.
Todo invisible en el lenguaje
Que se recuerda para vivir.

Regresó con la vieja montaña
Ilusión
La que nunca se encuentra jamás
Pero esta mañana cuando la subía
Era tan bonito el camino al andar.

ABOUT THE AUTHOR

Victor Hernández Cruz is the author of *Red Beans, Mainland, Tropicalization, By Lingual Wholes,* and *Rhythm, Content and Flavor.* He was featured on Bill Moyers's *"Language of Life"* series, and has received numerous awards including the Guggenheim Fellowship and the New York Poetry Foundation Award. In Granada, Spain, he gave a reading and talk at El Palicio de la Madraza, and in Madrid, stayed at La Residencia de Estudientes where he gave a reading of his poems and participated in a round table discussion sponsored by La Fundation Federico Garcia Lorca. He also read at the Universidad de Alcala at Henares in Cervantes' home town. He lives in Puerto Rico and writes in Spanish and English, and keeps a keen eye on avocados.